"There is joy in discovering the tru[...]
experience. Elizabeth Mattis Namgyel takes us on a personal exploration of the Buddha's most essential insight: *pratityasamutpada*—a.k.a.
dependent arising."

—Pema Chödrön, author of *Living Beautifully*

"*The Logic of Faith* looks into how we tend to seek comfort in ideas,
even though they can't provide real comfort. Elizabeth beautifully
illuminates the possibility of getting free from the prison of our
ideas, by softening into uncertainty and developing real faith. A
rich and helpful book."

—Sharon Salzberg, author of *Lovingkindness* and *Real Love*

"The beauty of this book lies in its remarkably creative presentation
of this insight of dependent arising. The author brings this fundamental insight of the Buddha to life for the contemporary reader."

—Thupten Jinpa, author of *A Fearless Heart*

"*The Logic of Faith* by Elizabeth Mattis Namgyel is a book that Americans who identify as spiritual-but-not religious and also those who
are practicing people of faith will find helpful. As a contemporary
American who has devoted herself to the most profound teaching
and practices of Tibetan Buddhism, she is uniquely poised to trans-
late esoteric and subtle [...] language that is accessible and
inviting. Elizabeth's la[...] ndly—as
it is with the most he[...] ality and
religion, reading Elizab[...] a conversation with a good frie[...]

—Rt. Rev. Marc Andrus, Bishop of the
Episcopal Diocese of California

*Audio versions of the analytical meditation
instructions found in this book can be accessed at*
www.shambhala.com/logicoffaithmeditations.

The Logic of Faith

A BUDDHIST APPROACH TO FINDING
CERTAINTY BEYOND BELIEF AND DOUBT

Elizabeth Mattis Namgyel

FOREWORDS BY
Thupten Jinpa *and*
Dzigar Kongtrul Rinpoche

SHAMBHALA • Boulder • 2018

SHAMBHALA PUBLICATIONS, INC.
4720 Walnut Street
Boulder, Colorado 80301
www.shambhala.com

Parts of the Belief section in chapter 3 were previously published in
Elizabeth Mattis Namgyel's article "Something to Believe In,"
Shambhala Sun, November 2012.

9 8 7 6 5 4 3 2 1

First Edition
Printed in the United States of America

♾ This edition is printed on acid-free paper that meets the
American National Standards Institute Z39.48 Standard.
♻ This book is printed on 30% postconsumer recycled paper.
For more information please visit www.shambhala.com.

Distributed in the United States by Penguin Random House LLC and in
Canada by Random House of Canada Ltd

Designed by Lora Zorian

LIBRARY OF CONGRESS CATALOGING-IN-PUBLICATION DATA

Names: Mattis Namgyel, Elizabeth, author.
Title: The logic of faith: a Buddhist approach to finding certainty
beyond belief and doubt / Elizabeth Mattis Namgyel.
Description: First Edition. | Boulder: Shambhala, 2018. |
Includes bibliographical references and index.
Identifiers: LCCN 2017022627 |
ISBN 9781611802306 (pbk.: alk. paper)
Subjects: LCSH: Religious life—Buddhism. | Belief and doubt.
Classification: LCC BQ5405 .M388 2018 | DDC 294.3/444—dc23
LC record available at https://lccn.loc.gov/2017022627

ODE TO GRACE

I pledge allegiance to the experience of grace, the expression of human insight from which all authentic faith traditions have arisen. I pledge allegiance to Mother Emptiness, *prajnaparamita*, to the wisdom of the Buddha, and the great spiritual genius, Nagarjuna. First and foremost, I pledge allegiance to my beloved teacher, Dzigar Kongtrul Rinpoche, who introduced me to the teachings of *pratityasamutpada*, which inspire me to continue my inquiry into the logic of not knowing and the pursuit of grace.

CONTENTS

FOREWORD

Thupten Jinpa

I am delighted to be invited to offer a foreword to Elizabeth Mattis Namgyel's delightfully engaging book *The Logic of Faith: A Buddhist Approach to Finding Certainty Beyond Belief and Doubt*. Despite its seemingly simple language, the book addresses some of the most challenging questions of spirituality—the nature of faith, its relation to human reason, and their roles in opening the gateway to awakening, as well as the fundamental question of the relationship between our perception and reality. In taking the role of critical inquiry, or *analytic meditation*, as part of the path seriously, I see this book as an important and timely corrective to the growing trend within contemporary writings on Buddhism, many of which tend to ignore the more proactive approach of what the Buddhist tradition calls the "wisdom aspect" of the path.

A central theme of this book is the notion of *dependent origination*, or dependent arising, which the author correctly characterizes as one of the most important insights of Buddhism. The early Buddhists understood this principle in terms of "mere conditionedness," offering a way of understanding both our own existence as well as the world's, not as something predestined but simply through the coming together of causes and conditions. As the profound implications of the principle of dependent arising came to be explored more deeply, it became recognized as revealing nothing short of the true nature of everything. In fact, in a scripture in the Pali Canon, we read the following statement attributed to the Buddha:

He who sees dependent arising sees the Dhamma; he who sees the Dhamma sees dependent arising.

It is no wonder then that, in his *Treatise on the Middle Way*, the influential second-century Buddhist thinker Nagarjuna singles out the teaching of dependent arising as the rationale for his paying homage to the Buddha. Following in his footsteps, the Tibetan master Tsongkhapa also wrote an entire eulogy to the Buddha for his teaching of dependent arising.

What then is this principle of dependent arising? Why so much fuss, one might ask? The Sanskrit term rendered as "dependent arising" is *pratityasamutpada*, which literally means "arising through dependence and in a related manner." The idea here is that while things arise in dependence upon some other factors, they do so not in isolation but within a web of deeply interconnected complexity. The Buddha illustrates this dependence with the imagery of two bundles of reeds leaning up against each other, such that when one is knocked over the other too would instantly fall. Thus, our author's characterization of dependent arising as *leaning* is spot on. Buddhist thinkers take great pains to explain that the two terms, *dependent* and *arising*, should not be understood as having a sequential relationship, as in the statement, "I washed my face and had breakfast." It is not the case that things first enter into a dependent relationship with each other and then arise or come to being. Rather, *dependence* and *arising* should be understood as being simultaneous, as in the statement, "I am going by flying," wherein the two verbs do not refer to two separate sequential acts.

This notion of dependence, at the heart of the Buddhist view of dependent arising, can be understood at different levels. At the basic level, there is the *causal dependence* in that nothing arises without dependence on their causes and conditions. This basic-level meaning is captured in the Buddha's well-known statement:

When this exists, that exists; from the arising of this, that arises.

This is also the meaning of the celebrated verse, known as the heart of dependent arising:

All things arise from their causes,
and the Tathagata taught what those causes are;
also that which puts an end to these causes—
this too was taught by the great monk.

There is, however, a further level of meaning to the notion of dependence, whereby dependence permeates the entirety of everything, not just their origination but even their very identity. The idea here is this: Even the seemingly simple concept of fire, for instance, presupposes an entire backdrop of experience, convention, language use, and conceptual framework, which includes our assumptions about its relation to fuel, function of burning, and so on. Seen this way, cause and effect are mutually dependent, with one defining or leaning on the other. In this sense, dependent arising becomes a most radical principle. It states that every single concept we have is utterly contingent, and the notion of an independent entity with its own identity with defined boundary is simply untenable. Everything is leaning on something else in such a way that to speak of things and events as if they possess some kind of autonomy necessarily involves falsification and gross approximation.

Thus for someone like Nagarjuna, dependent arising is both the *reason* as well as the *conclusion* of critical inquiry into the nature of reality. Things and events are devoid of intrinsic existence *because* they are dependent originations. At the same time, things and events *are* dependent arising; for independent existence and identity are utterly untenable. Nagarjuna in fact suggests an equation between emptiness and dependent arising, and states this is indeed the true Middle Way (*Treatise on the Middle Way*, 24:18). This stanza is perhaps the inspiration behind the well-known Zen saying that first one sees mountain as mountain and water as water; then one sees mountain as not mountain and water as not water; and, finally, one sees mountain as still mountain and water as still water. The point is not that, as a result of insight, one sees nothing; one still sees mountain as mountain and water as water, but this time, without the false assumption of there being intrinsically real entities behind labels we use to speak about them. If you want, one sees the same world without the filters and the blinders we project, but we see the world as it is—vibrant, present, and deeply interconnected.

Nagarjuna and his tradition never viewed the teaching on emptiness and dependent origination to be simply a matter of philosophy. For them the insight into this truth of dependent arising constitutes the very heart of the path to true awakening. As Nagarjuna puts it, the purpose of emptiness is to bring about the cessation of conceptual elaboration, which lies at the root of our grasping, psychological imprisonment to a solidified notion of reality, and emotional reactivity in our relationship with the world around us. And this undoing of our habitual grasping, grounded in our fixation to an objectifiable self and world, requires the serious business of critical questioning into the very roots of our habituation and its mechanism, so that we learn to view and relate to ourselves and the world in a way that is closer to the messy truth of profound interdependence. The seventh-century Buddhist master Chandrakirti, an influential interpreter of Nagarjuna, shows this point in the following:

> The wise ones have declared that the cessation of conceptualization / is a fruit of engaging in analysis. (*Entering the Middle Way*, 6:117cd)

The beauty of this book by Elizabeth Mattis Namgyel lies in its remarkably creative presentation of this insight of dependent arising. Constantly relating to our everyday experience and gently guiding through a series of self-inquiry, as well as drawing on insights from contemporary science, psychology, as well as literature, the author brings this fundamental insight of the Buddha to life for the contemporary reader. Approached in this manner, there is the real possibility that, as expressed by the author, the logic of emptiness, the uncovering of the complex layers of dependent relations embedded in reality, will no longer remain confined to the exclusive domain of academic scholarship. The individual's own reality becomes the field of inquiry, and the truth revealed through such an inquiry reflects nothing but the complex web of interrelationships that is the fact of one's existence. If embodied in this manner, the insight into dependent arising can offer anyone, whether Buddhist or not, a truly liberating perspective. Our habitual, rigid dichotomies of self and other, inner and outer, subject and object, and so on, naturally dissolve, and we begin to see and live our life in tune with the way things really are. So, as an enthusiast of the Buddha's teaching on dependent arising and as someone who aspires to embody this truth in everyday life, it is a real joy to introduce to the contemporary reader this beautiful book that helps bring the truth of dependent arising out in such a vibrant and refreshing way.

Thupten Jinpa
Principal translator to H.H. the Dalai Lama and author of
*A Fearless Heart: How the Courage to Be Compassionate
Can Transform Our Lives*

FOREWORD
Dzigar Kongtrul Rinpoche

In her book *The Logic of Faith*, Elizabeth Mattis Namgyel presents the central Buddhist principle of *pratityasamutpada*, or dependent arising, in a way that is completely original. I appreciate how she successfully combines the spirit and authenticity of the Buddha's teachings with the language and mind-set of the twenty-first century. Hers is not merely a conceptual understanding but reflects insight that has emerged from many years of serious study and practice.

Pratityasamutpada is a subtle but powerful teaching that lies at the heart of all the Buddha's teachings, transcending time and culture. Always relevant, because it is the key to gaining insight into the nature of how things are beyond dogma and beliefs, pratityasamutpada leads to a full understanding of all one needs to know. As Nagarjuna said, "One who knows dependent arising knows the dharma; one who knows the dharma knows dependent arising."

I have known Elizabeth for a long time, as a student and as my wife. She has a magnificent, open, and curious mind, which never ceases to look into everything. She loves the teachings on pratityasamutpada—that is clear—and her longing to share her enthusiasm with others in this book is evident. I have watched the teachings of pratityasamupada come to life in her, fulfilling her aspiration to be able to rest in wonderment of the nature of phenomena and the clear light of wisdom. This is surely the result of understanding the profound wisdom of interdependent origination, the nature of all things, which has no substantial reality whatsoever.

I hope this book will contribute to the authentic dharma taking root in the West so that genuine wisdom dawns in all who seek it.

PREFACE

As a child, I remember walking alone to the church a few blocks from my house to light candles. I didn't have a firm idea about to whom I was offering them. I had no concepts about faith or any shoulds or shouldn'ts, dos and don'ts, surrounding spirituality. I just felt attracted to the light. The experience of awe and humility that I sometimes encountered inspired this early impulse to devotion and aroused in me a longing to express it. I intuitively understood that this was something that arose deep within the nature of my being, and it didn't occur to me to name it.

Whether as a child or as an adult, we are all susceptible to moments when we emerge from our habitual reality. In these moments, we glimpse the magnificence of the world around us. And yet, as we grow into our lives, we are also susceptible to a world that others define for us.

Don't get me wrong. I am not dismissing the importance of language or the way other people think. We rely on others to help educate us about how to navigate the world we encounter. However, throughout all of this inevitable indoctrination, I feel fortunate that I continue to trust and pursue an experience too full for the likes of words, definitions, or labels.

The allegiance I have to this experience that I will call *grace* here, for the sake of talking about it, has led me on an active ongoing search, both within and outside the boundaries of my own mind. At the heart of this search lie questions, such as, "What incites these momentary experiences of well-being? Why do they come and go? And when I don't feel them, does this mean something is lacking in me? Do I lack faith?" It wasn't until my early twenties when I encountered the teachings on dependent arising—pratityasamutpada (pra-tee-tya-sam-ut-pada) in Sanskrit—that I slowly began to find words that spoke directly to these questions.

I received my first teaching on pratityasamutpada while sitting on a hill in a small Nepalese village named Dhulikhel, which overlooked an expansive and misty valley. I sat there quietly, alongside my teacher Dzigar Kongtrul Rinpoche (whom I had just recently met), unaware that he was about to introduce me to something that would in time completely blow open my world.

As I gazed out over green terraces of rice fields and tiny clusters of mud houses below, Rinpoche turned toward me and, holding up his hands with the tips of his two index fingers pressing together in a way that created a triangular roof-like shape, asked: "Lizzy, is this [the shape] one or two?"

I thought it was some kind of a trick question. "One or two *what?*" I wondered. I looked at the triangle and saw two fingers composing the shape, so I could not say that this (the shape) was *one* thing. And yet, I couldn't say the triangle was two either. So I replied, "Not one or two, not the same or separate."

To my astonishment, my new teacher seemed extremely pleased with me, although I wasn't sure why. It took me many years to understand the significance of his mysterious gesture and how it had any relevance to spiritual awakening. In any event, it turned out that this very lesson addressed, in the most exacting manner, some burning questions I'd had about faith and the experience of grace since I was a child. I won't try to explain the deep implications of this gesture to you now, but by the end of this book, I hope that you see the profundity of this simple teaching too.

Between the time I received this initial instruction and the time its wisdom began to dawn in me, I had a lot of learning—and unlearning—to do. It turns out that I had adopted some unexamined assumptions about spirituality—some beliefs and doubts. As I formally entered the Buddhist path I began to grapple with them.

First and foremost, I observed a misunderstanding in myself that I have come to understand as a form of fundamentalism.

This fundamentalism became apparent in moments when I felt there was no room for inquiry. At such times I felt that faith was something I was supposed to have—that as a "good" Buddhist I was expected to hold prescribed beliefs and feel unwavering certainty.

And yet, many questions would arise, such as, what was I to do when I didn't feel inspired by my meditation practice; when, as much as I wanted to feel compassion, my heart felt like a dry seed; or when someone in my spiritual community did something that challenged my values? Sometimes the conflict I felt was inspired by some rigid language I encountered in a particular translation of a text or from a run-in with someone else's narrow views. At such times, I began to associate faith with subtle forms of shoulds and shouldn'ts—sometimes hard-edged rights and wrongs. Whenever I looked at my experience through this limited lens, I watched the liveliness drain out of my spiritual practice. And this bothered me profoundly.

This all struck me as a contradiction. Didn't the Buddha famously encourage his disciples to trust their own process of awakening, when he said to them, "Don't simply believe what I say out of respect. Examine my words as a goldsmith examines gold"? As I wrestled with my own and others' spiritual ideals I often wondered, "Where has the child in awe of its fathomless universe gone?"

Well, it turns out that these dry spells—the times I assumed I lacked faith because I couldn't reconcile my ideals with my experience—have always been instrumental for any spiritual maturity to take place in me. I suspect this might be the same for you too. You might, like me, resonate with the words of the German theologian Paul Tillich, who said that doubt is an element of faith. Spirituality has no utility if it runs counter to life as we experience it. Let's face it: when the rubber meets the road, what use is the spiritual path if it doesn't address the human condition? What use is any endeavor that attempts to skirt life's dilemmas rather than look directly at them?

I have come to understand that, in order to evolve as a human being, I most certainly have some work to do. To live in grace has required me to look at the shoulds and shouldn'ts I've had about spirituality in order to engage a much livelier and direct approach. And yes, I inevitably move in and out of the experience of grace, but I find that I don't lose my way if I continually pursue it. In fact, I might even call the pursuit of grace faith.

ACKNOWLEDGMENTS

I would like to express my sincere and heartfelt gratitude to everyone who has stood behind *The Logic of Faith*. First and foremost, I want to thank my teacher, Dzigar Kongtrul Rinpoche, and the ancient lineage of Buddhist wisdom that flows through him. He has imparted the essential insight of dependent arising to interested students over the course of many years and has done so with intense passion, fierceness, and clarity. Someone once commented that receiving teachings on the Middle Way from Rinpoche is like trying to drink water from a fire hose. I know what she means.

Dave O'Neal, my editor at Shambhala Publications, nudged me in a particular direction when he suggested I write about the Middle Way teachings in the context of faith—a topic I was deeply exploring at the time. It turned out to be a mighty combo. I thank Dave for his vision and elegant way with language. He has been an advocate every step of the way.

I also want to thank Sasha Dorje Meyerowitz, my friend and writing buddy, also a devotee of the Middle Way teachings, for pushing at my language assumptions and making sure I said exactly what I meant. He is a creative and skilled communicator, and the book would not be as it is without him.

Additionally, I have three special friends to thank: Buddy Frank, Tatjana Krizmanic-Meyerowitz, and Owsely Brown for their invaluable kindness, encouragement, and support on every level.

Deep gratitude to the illustrious scholar Thubten Jinpa for his beautiful and thoughtful foreword, a teaching unto itself; and to Joanna Macy, who pops up a lot in this book. Her passion for and writings on the topic of pratityasamutpada have been a huge inspiration to me.

Much appreciation to dear Julia Sanderson letting me finish the book in her beautiful NYC apartment; Ani Lodro, my consultant on all things science; Greg Seton for his help in translating Tibetan and Sanskrit words; and Sue Kochen and Deborah Haynes for their ongoing encouragement and friendship. Thanks to Abba Hatcher and Gretchen and Chris Holland for their ongoing support. And of course, thank you to everyone at Shambhala Publications: Nikko Odiseos, Hazel Bercholz, KJ Grow, Kay Campbell, and Breanna Locke for bringing this all together, and to LS Summer for creating the index.

Lastly, my gratitude to Uma Devi, my grey mare and devoted friend, with whom I took long contemplative rides through the planes of the San Luis Valley during my writing breaks! I could say that those were the times I actually wrote this book!

THE LOGIC OF FAITH

Introduction

THE F-WORD

This entire book hinges on the word *faith*. You may assume that you know what that means. You may think that it has a single, clear definition. But words are not definitive structures: one word can have limitless—even opposing—meanings. Language morphs over time, and words take on different meanings depending on their contexts. You'll likely find as many definitions of faith as there are people to define it. Try asking around.

Just to give you an idea of some of the possible usages for the word *faith*, look at a standard English dictionary, which will most likely include in the definition such terms as *dogma, religion, fundamentalism, doctrine* or *indoctrination, confidence, trust, conviction,* and *spiritual insight,* to name a few. People make strong statements about faith, such as, "Faith without doubt leads to moral arrogance" or "If you don't have unwavering faith in God, you will go to hell." Some people feel that those who claim to have faith are deceiving themselves. These people equate faith with the disempowerment that results from blindly handing over agency to an authority figure. For others, faith describes the highest expression of human consciousness that transports us beyond the petty concerns of mundane life. Upon reflection you may notice that you use the term *faith* in various ways. But notice too that these varied usages have one thing in common: they reflect the desire to find ease in a world you can't secure.

Do you think it would even be possible to live in the world without faith? Because we rely on life around us, it seems to me we have no choice but to have faith. The late Buddhist teacher Thinley Norbu Rinpoche linked faith to the nature of existence when he said, "Cows have faith in grass."[1] This statement may seem simplistic at first glance, but it has deep implications. You cannot remove faith from the equation of your earthbound relative condition. That you depend on the world in which you live keeps you living in faith, and there is no way around it.

Given the multiplicity of definitions one finds around faith and given how crucial it is to our very existence, faith is worthy of deep consideration.

THE END OF FAITH?

At some point, after an extended period of exploring faith through personal practice and study, I decided to bring my investigation out into the world to see what others thought. I quickly learned that when I described my teaching topic using the word *faith*, no one was interested. In fact, once, when I was doing an online program on faith, someone wrote in on the chat, "This is just the mentality my grandmother had!" It was as though, by simply uttering the f-word, I had insulted his intelligence. For him faith was something that could only be outdated and backward. I have, by the way, noticed that the f-word does not generally go over well at Buddhist conferences either.

Subsequently, I started to call my inquiry "The F-Word"—and after that everyone wanted to talk. People are drawn to things that have a rebellious flare. And so I did what I had to do in order to draw attention to a topic that I feel is in desperate need of examination. As spiritual practitioners, scholars, and human beings looking for a sense of ease, it behooves us to reflect on the things that incite discomfort in us or that we don't understand, rather than simply buying into or rejecting them.

Many contemporary thinkers want to do away with the word

faith altogether and replace it with the term *spirituality*. In his book *The End of Faith*, Sam Harris links faith to terrorism, and reasonably so. People do unconscionable things in the name of faith. And yet I wonder, can we afford to do away with the word *faith* altogether? Personally I think that would be way too easy. I'm not saying the word *spirituality* doesn't have its use in the English language. But if you are not careful, spirituality can quite easily allow you to bypass the human dilemma, because spirituality can be anything you want it to be, whereas faith will challenge you. It's not so comfortable. It carries with it the undeniable tension between your search for security and the limits of your ability to know. Faith keeps your spiritual quest relevant and connected to the heart of the human predicament.

My concern also is that by narrowing the definition of faith to blind acceptance or dogma, we risk losing genuine traditions of contemplative wisdom and practice that include faith. The initial function of spirituality emerged from questioning the human condition and also from deep experiences of wonder. The word *religion* itself, initially meaning to "reconnect," seems to have come from direct experiences of something larger than just a set of fixed ideas. It marked a return to something essential that we just failed to recognize in the myopia of our everyday lives. How curious that we turn experiences of awe into dogmas and stagnant ideas. That we have come to associate faith with fundamentalism, blindness, and even terrorism gives us something important to look at.

PRATITYASAMUTPADA

So how does one look at faith—both as an experience and a cultural narrative—without closing down around dogmas and fixed ideas? I'm glad you asked. In this book I will introduce to you some methods of investigation that will address this very challenge. The basic approach we will take can be traced back to the very moment of the Buddha's awakening.

When the Buddha attained enlightenment beneath the Bodhi

tree in Bodh Gaya, India, he gained insight into the secret of the universe. It was from this insight that he revealed the powerful principle of pratityasamutpada, which is commonly known by its English translation, "dependent arising." Pratityasamutpada describes how everything we experience—both material and conscious—arises, plays out, and falls away in reliance upon an infinite web of contingent relationships. In other words, it is because things depend that life moves and we can experience it.

For those who study and practice the Buddha's path, his description of dependent arising has become a fresh and unimpeded way of perceiving mind and its world, and the primary understanding that makes liberation possible. It would be accurate to say that this very insight into the nature of dependent arising was the pivotal revelation of the Buddha, from which all of his subsequent teachings unfolded.[2] It was also the wisdom that my teacher was pointing out to me through his simple gesture years ago.

It is important for me to say, and for you to understand, that although pratityasamutpada comes to us through a formal continuum of Buddhist practice and realization, it is not a dogma or a set of ideas to adhere to. Instead the wisdom of pratityasamutpada functions like a portal into a completely new way of understanding your mind and its world, based on direct experience. It is a powerful insight that you can use as a tool to free yourself from the confusions you have about your place in the world in which you live. I know that sounds like a big promise, but such insight is quite simple and natural, I assure you. In fact, once you step outside your habitual way of seeing things, you will marvel at its obvious truth.

OPEN QUESTIONING

In the second century, the teachings on pratityasamutpada were revived and energized by the extraordinary spiritual genius Nagarjuna. He designed a series of methodical investigations based upon the Buddha's insight into the nature of dependent arising that provide a way for whoever employs them to bring together discerning intelligence with a mind of complete openness. The sole purpose of these investigations is to guide us away from the abstract realm of ideas into a direct relationship with life.

There is something important to be said here about the quality of the mind while engaged in a process of inquiry. I have often used the example of "the mind of an open question" to describe it. An open question—as opposed to a question intent on an answer—is one that has not settled on a conclusion or shut down around beliefs or doubts. Rather, when you ask an open question, you remain receptive, humble, and connected to the living and dynamic nature of things. According to this tradition, such characteristics describe a mind poised for insight. In fact, where insight is concerned, it is only an open and attentive mind that is said to perceive its object without mistake.

The purpose for saying all this here is to let you know in advance that I wrote this book as an inquiry, and so it will require some participation and curiosity on your part. In addition to sharing my experience, I will pose many questions for you and introduce several guided investigations that have been passed down by realized Buddhist masters skilled in the ancient art of meditative inquiry. I will invite you to voyage into your own experience of faith because—let's face it—there is no substitute for the certitude that results from seeing things directly for yourself.

To put it another way, what happens when we look at the world with fresh eyes and an open heart? Furthermore, what does it even mean to look here? How does one look? We will get into that in great depth. But for now, I just want to introduce the idea of dependent arising, pratityasamutpada, as your tool for exploring faith. And I want to make sure that you understand that although the methods used in this book come from the tradition of the Buddha, there is no assertion that insight itself is the possession of any one religion. We are all prone to moments of grace and clear seeing. And so, the term *insight*, as I use it here in this book, simply serves to describe an inherent potential in all of us.

Some of the methods presented in this book may challenge the assumptions you have about language, beliefs, doubts, spirituality, and the nature of knowing. They may bring to the fore some unexamined ideas you have about faith and even prompt you to rethink how you see yourself and the world in which you live. But then what's an exploration without challenges?

1

What Do I Know?

LESS RIGHT, MORE INFORMED

Our scientifically oriented knowledge seeks to master reality, explain it, and bring it under control of reason, but a delight in unknowing has also been a part of the human experience.

—Karen Armstrong, *The Case for God*

Chances are that knowing whether something is true or not is very important to you. You may often assume that the things you perceive or think are facts. So let me ask you this: Does knowing really ever capture truth? The term *knowing* describes your ability to perceive, be aware of, discern, or take in the world around you, but do you ever actually reach a final conclusion when it comes to knowing?

Every time I think I know something, it changes or I see it from another angle or another person's point of view. This suggests to me that the world doesn't lend itself to being known in a determinate way. And so, even after centuries of trying, we still have yet to find the ultimate cause for the creation of the universe or to agree upon an effective health care plan for all our citizens, and we certainly have never been able to reach a definitive conclusion to the age-old question "Who am I?"

Where does truth stand in a world that is dynamic and open to interpretation? In the realm of science, we continuously strive to discover new truths, which render old findings into building blocks

7

for new discoveries. Some contemporary scientists acknowledge the limitations of holding on to static truths. The theoretical physicist F. David Peat explains how in the realm of science it is widely held that certainty about the real world is a failed historical enterprise. In his book *From Certainty to Uncertainty* he writes,

> Scientific theory is a model of the real world, a model in which, for example, there is no friction, no air resistance, a model in which all surfaces are perfectly smooth and all motion is total uniform. It refers to a world where everything has been totally idealized.[1]

When ideas are set free into life, things get a bit messy and less predictive. It just will never be completely right. This is not to say that science doesn't make some amazing and useful discoveries. It only suggests that we can and do function in the world, regardless of whether something is true or not.

It seems to me that believing we know anything in a conclusive way serves only to impede our ability to discern and respond to life intelligently. Let me give you an example. I suspect that at one time or another (maybe in a situation when you're seated at a formal dinner and you can't get up to leave) you've been stuck talking to a "knower." Or should I say the knower has been talking to you, because knowers usually do most of the talking. Personally, I find it hard to pay attention to knowers with the force of all that truth flying at me. Rightness often comes with a lot of emotion. You may notice while talking to knowers that the intensity of their argument even makes them uncomfortable, and they often try to temper the "truth" of their statements by ending them with the phrase "But what do *I* know?"

I'm not castigating knowers. My encounters with knowers have caused me to reflect upon my own tendencies toward rightness. I've experienced the hangover after an evening of being right—the embarrassing aftermath of exposing the inflexibility of my thinking. I see how I failed to honor others' intelligence while at the same time finding myself at the mercy of their approval. When I leave myself vulnerable to others' opinions, I necessarily succumb to insecurity and a general loss of composure. Rightness has never provided me with the true confidence I seek.

To the same degree that I distrust all signs of rightness in myself and in others, I take pleasure in and cherish the qualities of humility, curiosity, and openness wherever and in whomever I encounter them. These qualities reflect an understanding of how to live in accord with the natural movement of life, and they express elegance and agility of being.

As much as you might share my appreciation for the qualities of humility and open-mindedness, you may still feel the need to hold on to at least some truths. "After all," you might ask, "don't we need strong principles in order to make decisive, responsible choices in life?"

This question itself reveals a subtle assumption one might have that open-mindedness is at odds with discernment. But if, in fact, you take the time to examine your experience, you may find that as you soften around your ideas, your mind becomes agile, and you can better connect with precision to the world around you.

Consider, for example, the process of an interview. Like me, you may have a favorite interviewer; mine is Terry Gross on National Public Radio's *Fresh Air*. I often look ahead for the topic of the guest she is interviewing later in the day. Occasionally, the topic doesn't interest me, but I decide to tune in anyway, while I clean the house or fold my laundry. As Terry teases open the interview, through her masterful process of gently guiding her guest in surprising and intimate directions, I find myself riveted by the intricacies of another person's story, the natural world, and the joys and challenges of the human condition. All of a sudden I begin to pay attention to the world around me in a new way. The single assumption I initially held about the topic cannot contain the liveliness of the discussion, which keeps opening and opening, never reaching a final destination other than the limits of airtime.

The unfolding of an interview is a useful example of how the unlimited and dynamic ways in which we perceive life are too rambunctious for the likes of right and wrong, is and is not, or singular ideas. That we can't capture the fullness of experience in thoughts doesn't make experience vague or abstract. Rather, a flexible mind brings us out of abstract ways of seeing things into a more nuanced relationship with life.

In this book we will explore the nature of knowing and whether or not we need to hold on to our truths in order to respond to life with acuity, efficacy, and vision. But just in case you are still wrestling with whether questioning truth might undermine your ability to function in the world, let me pose a question for you to consider: Is it not in the very moments you give over to the mystery and movement of life that you are able to experience your own brilliance?

GRACE IN RELATIONSHIP

When it all goes quiet behind my eyes, I see everything that made me flying around in invisible pieces. When I look too hard, it goes away. But when all goes quiet . . . I see I am a little piece in a big, big universe and that makes things right.

—The character Hushpuppy, from the film
Beasts of the Southern Wild

In 1968 the United States sent a manned spacecraft into orbit to circumnavigate the moon and explore the mysteries of the cosmos. These astronauts became the first in human history to travel beyond low earth orbit and look back at a fully illuminated earth from space. None of them had anticipated the transformative effect that such a glimpse would have on them. So impactful was the experience that those involved in the initial journey have wondered in retrospect if it may not have been the most important reason we went.

Since then many astronauts have described their experience of seeing earth from space as a sudden and unexpected recognition of interconnectedness: a decentering of the strong self-focused tendency we all have to put our self or our nation at the center of the universe. Astronaut Edgar Mitchell, who traveled to the moon in 1971, wrote books on his experience of this phenomenon, in which he chronicled not only his venture into space, but also how it served as the entry point into his personal exploration of human consciousness and the nature of self and its relationship to the universe. Mitchell described in a short film called *Overview* the effects of gazing out the window of the spacecraft at planet Earth as an alteration of his human perspective: "a kind of self-awareness that was not something new, but important to how we humans are put together."

Every great spiritual tradition has emerged from such human experiences of awe. As Mitchell suggested, this experience of self-awareness is not something new, nor is it exclusively for astronauts. And although we can't capture such encounters in words, we give them names: the grace of God, the Divine, buddha-nature, or the Tao. We have developed sophisticated systems of philosophy in an attempt to describe these experiences and have designed various methods of meditation and ritual to cultivate them. And all of these creative expressions—all the iconography, poetry, hymns, sacred architecture, and language—beautify our world; that is, of course, until we declare that our particular tradition is the one that really has it "right." This never fails to dampen the sense of wonder that initially inspired this creative expression in the first place.

Let's take care not to lose sight of the original purpose of our wisdom traditions by protecting them from rightness. Let's cherish them because their ultimate aim is to release us from our constant struggle to find sanity in a world we can't secure.

I remember vividly my first meeting with the accomplished Tibetan Buddhist teacher Dilgo Khyentse Rinpoche, when I was in my early twenties. He had an impressive history. In his teenage years, driven by his own longing, he left home to practice meditation alone in a cave for many years. He mastered all the lineages of Tibetan Buddhism—protecting and cherishing each of them according to their unique qualities while emphasizing their essential similarities. He escaped Tibet with his family during the Chinese Cultural

Revolution and settled in India. In time he assumed the position of spiritual advisor to the royal family of Bhutan and became the spiritual father of hundreds of young monks whom he tenderly raised in his monasteries in Nepal and Tibet.

He had a grand and elegant physical presence, and although he was in his midseventies when I first met him, he didn't seem confined by time, age, or even gender. Before entering his room I had pictured him as a wise old man from whom I would receive spiritual guidance. But to my astonishment, as I entered his quarters, what struck me most—and how I remember him to this day—was how he embodied, more than anyone I had ever met, the spirit of amazement. He did not live in some distant state of meditative absorption. Rather, he seemed touched and delighted by everything and everyone around him, and he responded to it all with curiosity, playfulness, and gentleness. In that moment I thought, "This must be where the spiritual path leads."

I suspect you have had moments when your world opened up and you felt completely resolved and free. You may have encountered such occurrences while engaging a spiritual practice, while listening to an inspiring piece of music, or while walking alone in the mountains after a snowfall. Sometimes insight and confidence can surprise you in the midst of a crisis, stirring you awake from the core of your being. At other times, a brief encounter with a stranger on the subway might be all it takes to shake you out of the tired and familiar world you live in. And you may, for a while, find yourself moving playfully through life without fear.

You might describe such a happening as a deep, melancholic sigh that releases compassion and tenderness; a fierce, unshakable confidence; or a surrender to an intense longing that feels both unconsummated and utterly fulfilled at the same time. Such moments of genuine insight provide a respite from the landscape of insecurity, distraction, and fear in which you may often live: all the shutting down, pushing away, feeling overwhelmed, and all the neurotic attachment. You may notice that in such instances your habitual mind relaxes, allowing you to enjoy the rich, dynamic energy of life. You may call this a religious experience, but also a deeply human one. You might even call it grace.

In spiritual contexts we often think of grace as something that is bestowed upon us. Once when giving a talk at Harvard Divinity School, I was asked to define grace in the tradition of the Buddha. "Is grace something," a man asked, "bestowed upon us from the outside—from a divine presence? Or is it something inherent within the mind itself? What is the role of grace or divinity in the nontheistic tradition of Buddhism?" This question led to a lively discussion and has continued to illuminate my own practice and understanding.

In the spirit of the Buddhist tradition, I suggested that grace comes from finding your place in relationship to the world around you. You may often wait for someone or something to bequeath grace upon you. It may appear that it takes an extraordinary or sacred external event to evoke an experience of grace. But your very ability to recognize something outside of yourself and see its value forms part of the equation of grace. The qualities of appreciation and humility, which arise as natural expressions of your own mind, are no less sacred than the objects that arouse them. To be touched by the beauty and pain of life rather than trying to live around them creates grace.

All this is to say that grace doesn't happen in a vacuum but rather from the intercourse between your awareness and the world you encounter. Grace happens when you find yourself in sane relationship with your world.

EVERYTHING LEANS

If you can prove a statement one-hundred percent true, it does not describe the world.

—Bart Kosko paraphrasing Einstein, *Fuzzy Thinking*

There have been those who have challenged the certitude of their thoughts and perceptions throughout history. Particularly at the turn of the twentieth century, the developments in microscopic and telescopic technologies blew open our perceptual strategies, radically changing our perceptions in fields such as science, philosophy, religion, and art.

Only a decade or two earlier, during the mid-nineteenth century, a small group of French artists began to question the way they saw things. These painters, later known as impressionists, began including in their work the many interdependent factors that influenced the way they represented their visual environment. They had to move quickly to take in the constant changes in form, movement, and light, a departure from the techniques of traditional art of the time. Instead of emphasizing precision, detail, and the modeling of form as the realists did, they painted with dabs of color, using visible brushstrokes, accentuating the effects of the passage of time, movement, and the dimensionality of ordinary subject matter, as crucial elements of human perception.

I once went to an exhibition at the Grand Palais in Paris, featuring a collection of some of Monet's greatest works. The museum had dedicated several rooms to a good number of Monet's renditions of the Rouen Cathedral, which he painted at more than thirty distinct times of the day and year. What struck me as I slowly meandered through the chambers of the museum was how the paintings reflected his faithfulness to the observed world—as if he honored each moment of perception, chasing the effects of light, dimension, and the changing atmosphere of his own mood. Monet was part of a growing movement that placed less emphasis on what they were seeing than how they were seeing. His paintings convey the never-ending continuum of change in form and of his perception of it—the coming together and falling away of the infinite elements that comprise each moment of experience.

Our world keeps changing, and we change right along with it. Bart Kosko's statement at the beginning of this section describes this well. The fact that you can't pin down truth doesn't make your perceptions or thoughts vague or muddled. Monet's paintings are a tribute to that. It's just that as much as you attempt to know things with certainty, life continues to burst from the seams of your beliefs and ideas.

You may think that your inability to capture truth is due to limitations of your basic intelligence: that there are answers "out there" but you have yet to find them. Instead, I would suggest that there is a reason you can't know things in a definitive way, and it has to do with the nature of relationship.

The Buddha, at the time of his awakening, had a tremendous insight into the nature of relationship, and it was through this breakthrough that he revealed the secret of the universe through a concise and powerful formula:

This being, that becomes. From the arising of this, that arises. This not being, that becomes not. From the cessation of this, that ceases.[2]

The Buddha is referring here to the way in which all conscious and material experiences arise, express themselves, and fall away due to a multiplicity of causes and conditions. This is the natural principle we've identified as pratityasamutpada, or "dependent arising."

To illustrate dependent arising, the Buddha used the example of two bundles of reeds leaning up against each other. If one were to knock over one bundle, the other would naturally fall to the ground. Everything stands by virtue of something else: "This being, that becomes" and because this falls, that falls.

You can find many translations of the term *pratityasamutpada*: "dependent arising," "the great nature of contingency," "interbeing," "conditioned genesis," "interdependent origination," just to name a few. But all of these terms simply refer to the way in which all things express themselves through the nature of contingent relationships. In other words, it is because everything leans that the world moves and we can experience it.

We could simply use the term *relationship* to describe the principle of pratityasamutpada, but there is a common tendency to misunderstand the subtley of its meaning in this context. For instance, we often refer to someone being "in a relationship" when he or she is dating someone consistently. In other words, we see things or people as being sometimes in relationship and sometimes not. In the context of these teachings, however, everything is always in relationship. In fact, you could almost say that everything is made of relationship, in a sense.

All things—from the smallest particle of matter, to a moment of consciousness, to something as large and dense as a rock—arise, express themselves, and fall away in reliance upon others. Results are contingent upon causes; what we call a thing—be it conscious or material—is comprised of finer elements or moments; and a moment of cognition arises in dependence upon its corresponding object of perception.

In her book *World as Lover, World as Self*, the deep ecologist, environmental activist, and Buddhist scholar Joanna Macy translates *pratityasamutpada* as "mutual dependency" and describes it as "a reciprocal dynamic at play." The power of mutual dependency, she explains, is not controlled by one dominating entity but is rather the dynamic expression of relationships between all entities, and this makes everything happen.

In that everything leans, we cannot separate ourselves from the world we experience. For a moment, try to imagine yourself as a truly independent entity, with no relationship to anything whatsoever. If you were to reside outside of the nature of contingency, how would you perceive information through your senses, feel pain or pleasure, or communicate through language? You might ask yourself how you would even move, because movement itself requires a multiplicity of interrelated physical parts working together, searching for balance in the field of gravity.

Undoubtedly, you will find it impossible to even imagine being independent of the world around you because if you were truly independent—versus interdependent—you would be inert and couldn't experience anything at all. But don't just assume this is all true. Try to separate yourself from what you know, feel, think, see, hear, smell, and taste. When you see this is not possible, you will gain confidence in pratityasamutpada through your own direct experience.

Even if through investigation you find that you cannot separate yourself from the world you experience, you may still assume that because you identify things by their characteristics, they must have at least some independent truth or existence from their own side. So let me challenge this assumption by introducing a playful example, which may help you understand how the characteristics we assign to things depend upon their respective contexts.

If you were to compare a toothpick to a splinter—the kind you sometimes get in your finger—you would probably say that the toothpick is long and the splinter is short. But if you hold the toothpick next to a tree branch, you would have to say the toothpick is short by comparison. That the toothpick finds its size only in its relationship to other things shows that its size depends on context and thus has no inherent size of its own. You may argue that because most people identify the qualities of a toothpick in a similar way, it must have some kind of objective truth from its own side. But what we call a *toothpick* is a relative linguistic agreement based on the utility we designate to it.

In fact, I shyly admit that when I get obsessive about cleaning, I use toothpicks to get at the in-between places in my refrigerator and other appliances. Just because we call them *toothpicks* does not mean these things that most English speakers describe as bigger than splinters and smaller than tree trunks have intrinsic toothpick properties, such as size, sharpness, function, or name.

Because everything leans, the world doesn't lend itself to being known in a determinate way, and yet, as you can see, that doesn't mean that things lose their distinction. In fact, it shows us that things find definition, meaning, and utility only in relationship to other things. What does this show us? It shows us that what we think to be the case will always be a vague approximation of a fathomless play of interconnected relationships. When you think about things in this way, it may make you more attentive to the world and how you move about in it.

EMERGING FROM NOT NOTICING

It is my experience that the world itself has a role to play in our liberation. Its very pressures, pains, and risks can wake us up—release us from the bonds of ego and guide us home to our vast true nature.

—Joanna Macy, *World as Lover, World as Self*

Although you may not think about it as you move about your life, you have an intimate and natural relationship with pratityasamutpada. You observe the persistent linkage between cause and effect as you head to work each day in order to pay your bills; you know that if you drop a glass onto a hard surface, it will shatter; and when your car breaks down and you have to get it fixed, you probably don't think twice about the fact that it is made of parts. We all, at times, make careless choices without reflecting upon the consequences. For instance, we might subsist on coffee and doughnuts for years without conscious consideration of what it might do to the complex and responsive organism we call our body.

There is a Sanskrit term for this in Ayurvedic medicine: *prajna aparadha*. Prajna aparadha might be translated as actions that "undermine prosperity" or could be loosely defined as "crimes against wisdom." In certain spiritual contexts it refers specifically to breaking vows one has taken that keep one in the boundary of one's intention to awaken. Fundamentally, prajna aparadha alludes to the choices you make that dishonor your basic intelligence: from the times when the world gives you feedback but you don't pay attention, to the many moments you live in a state of myopia where you don't recognize yourself as an integral part of a sensitive and lively interconnected matrix.

Because everything leans, the world gives you feedback. You might use terms such as *feedback* or *karma* to describe the connection between specific causes and their results. But if you closely observe the nature of dependent arising, you will see everything as the reverberating effects of infinite elements coming together and falling away in each moment. How you as an individual experience this continuous movement comprises the flow of events you call your life.

Chances are some of these events pan out according to your preferences, and some of them don't. When you don't like where the chips fall, you might pinpoint a singular source of your misery. But in the broadest sense, there is nothing to blame but the dynamic play of infinite elements—the activity of the great web of contingency, of which you are an integral part.

Once you understand that this world of appearances and possibilities[3] is not limited to the way you perceive it, you might not get so hung up on your own truths. You may see firsthand how widening your lens works against your habitual tendency to shut down around knowing anything in a fixed or determinate way and how this leads you toward a less reactive and more responsive approach to things. As you trace how your choices and attitudes shape your life, you gain keen insight into the subtle yet vital patterns that influence your experiences of suffering and freedom.

In this book, we will continue to ask many questions concerning how to live in harmonious relationship with the world around us. We will look at the mechanics of falling in, and out, of grace. It is a given that human beings long for a sense of ease and meaning in life—that is not in question here. But how we strive for happiness needs to be deeply examined because the way we live our lives is often at odds with our deepest intentions.

In our quest for well-being we spend much time focusing on our individual needs, forgetting that our emotional and physical health is inextricably linked to the world in which we live. As we awaken from our self-absorption, we will see that there is no way to identify where we—as individuals—end and the world begins; we will see that we are, in fact, inextricably linked. As we begin to notice the world around us, our longing to let life touch us will increase, and we will respond naturally to others with a sense of kinship and tenderness.

By observing interdependence we emerge from the complacency of not noticing. For instance, recently a plethora of dramatic elemental happenings have shaken us awake as a global society: resource scarcity, severe changes in weather patterns, environmental toxicity.

Of course, there has never been a time when we haven't experienced the consequences of our actions. But in a broader collective sense, these global challenges are ushering us into a new awareness of the delicate and undeniable bond we share with our planet and other beings.

Part of the growing concern for the environment emerged when humans witnessed, for the first time, images of the earth as seen from space—a recent gift of perspective. The first photograph of a fully illuminated earth was taken on December 7, 1972, and remains possibly the most widely distributed photographic image in human history. Because of its glassy appearance, the image became affectionately known as the "Blue Marble."

Over the decades since the introduction of this visual reference, our relationship to the planet has changed dramatically. The image has revealed to us that the ground we stand on and the atmosphere that protects us from the powerful forces of the outer universe are more fragile than we had imagined. It has forced us to reflect upon the impact of human consumption and on the careless ways we have related to our surroundings. It continues to serve as an icon of a new global awareness that has energized an investigation into how we might protect rather than violate our relatively small and precious home.

The direct and undeniable feedback we receive from the imbalances in natural systems can change the way we understand human evolution. Rather than seeing evolution as a linear process of growth, we might consider whether human evolution may not have more to do with emerging from not noticing—a return to the wisdom traditions of our ancestors who recognized the intricate and reciprocal relationship they had with their world. Here I don't just mean the physical world—our planet—but also the way we live our lives and how we relate to everything we encounter.

Interdependence offers us a new way of looking at things by drawing us out of the narrow tunnel of self-absorption into a broader awareness. It shows us the way to live in sane relationship to our world, in grace. This understanding is not only inextricably linked with our survival but with basic sanity and insight as well.

DELUSION, REALNESS, AND ILLUSION

REAL: Designating whatever is regarded as having an existence in fact, and not merely in appearance, thought, or language: having an absolute, in contrast to a merely contingent, existence.

—*Oxford English Dictionary*

That everything leans implies a world of infinite connectedness. But it also implies that what we think of as the world is far from being a collectively agreed upon truth; rather, it is actually vastly distinctive in the myriad ways we individually perceive and interpret it. Have you ever imagined what it must be like to see the world through someone else's eyes? Or even through the eyes of another species? When you start to think in this way, certain questions may arise: If we experience things so dissimilarly, how do we establish or identify truth? How is it we make a distinction between delusion, reality, and illusion?

In a general sense, delusion refers to an inaccurate perception of reality. We can identify the symptoms of delusion in cases where someone experiences a reality in a way no one else does or when someone holds idiosyncratic beliefs that go against consensual agreements or commonly held realities of particular groups or societies. We often associate delusion with mental disorders. For instance, you may be casually riding the subway on your way to work, while someone sitting right beside you shows clear signs of experiencing a world full of danger that you don't see, where everything that person encounters seems to conspire against him or her.

Cases like that may be fairly clear-cut, but if you take a closer look, you may find that the line between reality and delusion is not so easy to locate. What does it mean for something to be real? What are the criteria for real? What seems real in your world? You may assume that real things are simply agreed upon facts. You may believe that something is real simply because you're the one experiencing it.

You may assign realness to objects that evoke in you strong feelings of excitement or rage, or think that because you experience their vividness, charge, and intensity, this is an indication that your feelings are real. You could argue that anything dense or solid to the touch is real—but then what about less substantial phenomena such as music, mist, or an experience of faith or awe? Would you say these things are real?

You may also use the term *real* to describe someone who you believe has the qualities of straightforwardness, who doesn't seem to have a hidden agenda, or who acts with a genuine motivation. You may ascribe realness to anything capable of performing a function, or you might ascribe realness to something comprised of one element, such as an object made of pure substances—"real gold." You may assume there is a standard for real, but in fact, do any of us ever see anything in exactly the same way? When you begin to look closely, it all gets a bit ambiguous.

When you consider that what is taken for reality depends upon a context, you may start to suspect that things don't have an objective existence at all. Another way of saying this is that things don't possess intrinsic characteristics from their own side. We establish reality based upon perceptions and consensual agreements. For instance, if I were to ask you to imagine "the world," what comes to mind? What do you see? You may have residual visual imprints from watching the morning news, or it might evoke personal images of your workplace, family, or the town in which you live. You may also recall collective images you have seen, such as the Blue Marble image. You may accept this universal image of planet Earth as the definitive visual reference for what the world is, but if you think about it, the perspective of seeing the image of a fully illuminated earth from space has only been available to us since 1972. In fact, there are still many people who have no concept that the world is round at all.

Once a woman in a remote area of Nepal asked me how far I had to walk to get to her village. I took out an orange to demonstrate the distance between our two "villages." But she had no idea what I meant because she had no concept of a round world. However, her ability to grow her own food and live simply with contentment showed me she had a deep and connected relationship to her world, no less right than mine.

Not all of Earth's creatures see the world as we humans do. A photographic image of the earth would mean nothing to a horse, a dog, or a bird. They have no longing or ability to step away from where they stand to see how it might look from a different vantage point. They occupy their time looking for grass and seeds, frolicking, and protecting themselves from danger. What we consider a true understanding of the planet—our luminous globe—is a human marvel. We might argue that we have the most accurate perception of the world because we have the ability to step away from things to gain perspective. We can look out at space through a telescope or penetrate deceptively solid boundaries through looking at life microscopically, and we can see the inside of the human body through an x-ray, but that doesn't mean that our view is the ultimate expression of how things are. As a species we look through a particular lens, driven by the human impulse to continually learn and discover new things. So there will never be the world—but rather a continuum of changing relative experiences that depend upon our particular point of view.

Please don't misunderstand me: I am not questioning the value of the inquisitive spirit or worthiness of scientific exploration and discovery—the joy, potential, and wonder of it. Nor am I eschewing the import of our collective human perceptions and agreements about our place in the cosmos. And I am certainly not refuting the common perception that the world is round (or elliptical). This is something we agree upon consensually. But I do recognize that even the notion of roundness is an agreement we humans hold about the way in which we see things as a species and what we name them. Furthermore, what we know of our planet and the universe is information that has been gathered in a cosmological millisecond and that it is far from conclusive. In the realm of science we have moved from a flat earth, to a round earth in a universe that has edges, to an expanding universe, to a multiverse, which, in turn, contains infinite multiverses, and so on, in a breathtakingly short time. We may have an insider's view or an outsider's view—the view of an expert or the view of a novice—but these truths we maintain will always remain just views.

In order to find an objective reality then by virtue of its truth, we would all have to experience things in exactly the same way. But we don't. We each have distinctive histories and biological and psychological makeups that change in each moment. We will always see the world unlike anyone else does, and even within the continuum of our own awareness we will never experience the same thing twice in exactly the same way. That we have such different experiences explains why there is a world full of creative expression, as well as a world full of conflict. And although we do have rare moments when we feel perfectly in sync with others' ideas, these moments never seem to last, and the differences continue to remind us that communication will always remain imperfect and incomplete.

Considering that we all experience life differently, it is a wonder that we can communicate at all. Yet we manage to find some orderliness and cohesion to make interaction happen. We can reference things and create systems that allow us to function consistently as groups and societies. We have developed languages to communicate with one another based on arbitrary sounds we call words. Language works because we collectively agree to connect words to particular objects or associate them with certain feelings or experiences. To speak of this reality independent of our description of it is meaningless. But that language doesn't possess an inherent truth doesn't seem to inhibit our ability to communicate effectively (at least to some degree). It doesn't prevent us from writing e-mails and poetry or expressing how we feel. In this way, language serves as a highly functional apparition. Although it possesses no inherent truth, it is one of the primary ways we are able to participate in life.

In the traditional Buddhist teachings, the great masters describe the phantasmagoria we call our life and world by using a series of metaphors: a rainbow, a magician's display, an echo, a dream, or a mirage.

In the unique town where I live, Crestone, Colorado, many spiritual communities have built temples and sacred monuments along the base of the Sangre de Cristo mountain range. Often, on rainy summer afternoons, if you eavesdrop just a little while standing in line at our local grocery store, you might hear disparate groups of people from these various communities saying, "Did you see the rainbow over our temple today?" Of course we all know, in fact, that the location of a rainbow always depends on where you stand. Positioning yourself at different vantage points you will see the rainbow in entirely different places. You can never drive through a rainbow or find its true location; rainbows are unfindable, insubstantial, without a speck of realness. Yet rainbows appear vividly to our senses as the play of contingent relationships. Like all things, they arise when specific causes and conditions come together and, in turn, will fade when these relationships change.

That things are illusory doesn't prevent a functioning and apparent world from arising and producing the fathomless display each of us uniquely experiences, with all its pain, beauty, and creative potential. That something doesn't intrinsically exist does not take away its potency or our ability to feel and experience it. Examples such as dreams and rainbows illustrate that things don't have to be real in order to function.

So here I want to make a distinction between illusion and delusion. In the context of these teachings, illusion refers to seeing through appearances by recognizing their interdependent nature. Delusion, on the other hand, refers to misapprehending things to have an independent reality from their own side. It is important to be able to make a distinction between the nature of things and the way in which they appear. Without developing some savvy about the mind and its world, we are often overtaken by what we assume to be real and get lost in the momentum of reactivity and rightness. To misperceive the illusory and ungraspable nature of our inner and outer worlds as real describes delusion in the context of teachings on pratityasamutpada. And in this sense, we are all a bit deluded, I'm afraid.

When threatened or injured, all animals draw from a "library" of possible responses. We orient, dodge, duck, stiffen, brace, retract, fight, flee, freeze, collapse . . . It is when these orienting and defending responses are overwhelmed that we see trauma.

—Peter Levine

One way in which you can observe the effect of clinging to things as real is through physical, emotional, and conceptual contraction. Contraction is not necessarily a problem in and of itself. For example, the heart has to contract to pump blood, and we need materials that compress and harden, such as cement, to build sturdy foundations. When we breathe, if our diaphragms didn't contract on the out-breath, how could they expand when we need to inhale? We could define *contraction* as the narrowing of boundaries, the compressing of energetic or material substances, or the congealing or thickening of conscious elements into ideas or beliefs. We contract when we withdraw or pull back from relationship.

All conscious creatures contract when afraid or threatened. A tortoise instinctually retreats into its shell for a reason. Contraction has a shielding and protective purpose in nature, but as a way of being in life, contraction can prevent us from feeling connected to the world around us. In this way we could say that contraction moves us in the opposite direction from the liberating insight of pratityasamutpada.

Most of us live in a state of contraction much of the time. Of course, because everything leans, no one can actually withdraw from the activity of interdependence, but we can—and so often do—brace ourselves against life. The dynamic energy of our world keeps moving, providing us with feedback, rattling our screws loose, and we respond by continually tightening them. Exhausting isn't it?

We call this experience of physical and energetic tension and anxiety *stress*. We contract when the overwhelming quantity of stress stuns us into inactivity or reactivity and prevents us from seeing outside the constricted boundaries of our thoughts and emotions. At times everything around us feels jagged and unfriendly, and the tiniest, most insignificant events seem huge and impossible, making us feel too small for our life. The contraction that results can restrict our perspective to such a degree that we literally withdraw from participating in and feeling our world.

You may notice that you have subtle ways of receding from life. Perhaps it shows up as feeling indifferent to everything that goes on around you so that at the end of each day nothing seems to have changed, as if your life hasn't touched you. You might get pulled by an urgent need for distraction, lose yourself in substance addiction, or binge-watch television. At times you might collapse into a frozen and immobilized state of fear, take on the impossible responsibility of keeping everyone else's emotional life together, or develop narcissistic patterns that hold you hostage in your own daily drama. Submerged in your own myopic realities you can go a lifetime assuming they are true.

Trauma is a strong word that we usually associate with extreme suffering. But trauma can also be insidious and hard to recognize. In fact, it is doubtful whether anyone gets through life without some trauma. We experience trauma when we can't remove ourselves from a dangerous or unhealthy situation or relationship, when we are overwhelmed by an unexpected catastrophic event, or when in our vulnerability or innocence we don't have the clarity and emotional strength to make sense of what surrounds us.

When unable to ingest and process experience, we develop beliefs about ourselves and the world that we carry into life. We generally think of beliefs as ideas, but in fact we hold beliefs in our emotional, energetic, and physical bodies as well. Our postures and the way we live mirror unconscious patterns of bewilderment that evolve around unexamined truths. We perceive the world, in turn, to reflect these patterns, affirming them and causing us to cling to the stories that arise about them.

For instance, due to a childhood trauma a person might walk

through life desperately wondering, "What about me?" He may continually perceive himself to be left behind or ignored. Another person might struggle with low self-esteem and feel diminished or ineffective and wonder why the world seems so harsh, why her relationships plague her, or why she struggles at work. While entrenched in our own confusion, we may not even question the basis of these realities, or if we do, we may often find it hard to see our way out of them. After a while they start to feel like the norm.

I bring this all up because in the practice tradition of dependent arising, as you shall see, we will question the rightness or truth of our beliefs. You might think that in the case of trauma to question your beliefs would be to dismiss or deny the trauma you have endured. But ask yourself this: Does questioning beliefs have to reduce your ability to respond to suffering? Does it necessarily prevent you from removing yourself from dangerous or unwholesome situations or imply that you should turn your back on illness, violence, or abuse? Human beings survive unconscionable suffering. Everyone has a story. I always feel astounded by what people go through and how resilient they can be.

But at times you may wonder if just surviving is enough and, if it's not, what you might do about it. If you want to emerge from confusion, you will have to explore the deep-rooted assumptions you have about your mind. You will need to identify your beliefs, question them, and see how they drive you. And as right as you may assume you are about yourself, your relationships, and the events of your life—even if an army of people agrees you have been wronged—you will still have to examine the truth or realness of your stories and see how they do or don't serve you.

In a sense, exploring your beliefs can be compared to venturing outside the security of your home to see how the world works. You may have to distance yourself from the familiar in order to open yourself to a larger discovery. When you begin to flirt with the idea that perhaps there is life outside your story, you may have the liberating insight that however stuck you may feel and as dark as things may seem, stuckness is not even a possibility in a world whose only reliable characteristics are movement and change. In fact, when you pause and look more closely at things, you may discover that all these beliefs that seem to haunt you and cause you so much grief actually share one spectacular and redeeming quality: they are not true. In other words, you are not doomed.

BEYOND APPEARANCES

Don't let the appearance of things outshine their nature.

—Dzigar Kongtrul Rinpoche

As you begin to examine your core beliefs, it may surprise you to discover how profoundly you give yourself over to appearances— that you don't generally question them or even entertain the idea of looking at how you get caught in the realness of your stories. My teacher, Dzigar Kongtrul Rinpoche, describes this as the confusion of "the appearance of things outshining their nature."

When we get angry, for instance, a false sense of certainty arises regarding the object we consider a threat or the cause of our aggression. Anger has its own logic. Your roommate leaves his clothes on the floor: "Doesn't he care? Doesn't he see that I live here too?" An unsettling sensation erupts from the depths of your being, and your engine begins to rev up, like when you accidently step on the gas pedal while your car is in park: vroom . . . It starts off slow and takes on speed and momentum. Vroom, vroom . . . Images of your roommate's negligence flash before your eyes. Patterns of behavior come into focus: dishes in the sink, crumbs on the counter, that moldy thing in the refrigerator. "Did he expect me to clean that? Why does all the responsibility always fall on me?" Vroom, vroom, vroom!

The plot thickens, gathers momentum. Things are moving fast. You feel kind of flushed and have to remove your sweater. It all starts to fit together; the story starts to congeal. How could you have missed what should have been so obvious? Vroom . . . You were asleep to the whole dynamic! Vroom! The energy of this new emerging paradigm comes into focus. You are now riding high on the clarity of your logic, and although you might say the situation doesn't please you, being right feels invigorating—alive even. You observe a renewed sense of purpose and certitude in your life. Vroom!

At this point in the game, because you have all the proof you need to make your case, you probably won't question the nature of your agitation or the way you see your roommate. Why would you? To investigate the situation further would be to dismiss patterns of behavior you see with your own two eyes—it would betray the trust you have in your own discernment. Never! You have the evidence directly in front of you—his clothes are literally strewn about the floor. This provides just the ammunition you need to carry out your plan: he has one month's notice to find another place.

But wait. Why don't you pause here for a moment—before you send that angry e-mail or leave that nasty note—and ask yourself a question: "Do I feel completely comfortable with the direction this is taking?" If your answer is no, let's back up a bit and trace how this all evolved.

Before you realized the truth about your roommate—before that initial spark we call a thought took hold in you—what were you doing? Maybe you were preparing to go outside. And maybe you felt pretty good too. Then, as you were about to get your shoes, you almost tripped on his clothes. You could have done just about anything—it was a moment of limitless potential. Instead, it became a moment of confusion. You lost the bigger picture, and your thoughts ran with his dirty laundry proliferating into a full-blown, ever-expanding hyperbolic universe, fortified by strong emotions and a seamless story. But it doesn't look so seamless now. In fact, as you reflect back it looks flimsy, arbitrary, and—frankly—utterly distorted. This new reality of yours was a quantum leap from getting ready to go outside for a stroll. You begin to entertain a bit of doubt regarding the rightness of your story. Maybe you shouldn't send him that nasty e-mail after all.

While deep in thought you stray into the kitchen. Lo and behold, there he stands—your roommate—innocently holding a cup of coffee he has just made: for you. He has no idea where you've been. He doesn't look at all as if he's out to wreck your life. Perhaps he's not such a horrible person after all. In his simple and kind gesture the power of your reasoning instantly erodes, and you remember that he is, in fact, your best friend.

This is all well and good, but you may still have a lingering issue: he hasn't picked up his clothes. What do you do now? Just suck it up? Before, when he was the antagonist in your drama, the solution was easy: you had to protect your turf. But now as he's your best friend again, is it wrong to push the issue? This ambiguity throws you off your game, and you begin to doubt your perceptions—your discernment—altogether.

You may interpret this lack of exactness as a loss of direction, but would it have been better to try to solve the problem from a state of unwavering rightness—when you had a false sense of confidence concerning the situation? Perhaps this uncertainty brings you closer to the true nature of your roommate: you can't make him completely right, and yet you can't make him wrong either. Yes, you can identify patterns of behavior you may need to address, but various causes and conditions seem to dictate the flow of the situation, like that cup of coffee. Things keep changing, and your thoughts and perceptions change right along with them, forcing you to include disparate perceptions into what you formerly thought was a "sure thing."

The Buddhist scholar and philosopher Herbert Guenther had a term for the unknowable nature of things and the mind that perceives it. He called it "open-dimensionality." If you put your attention to it, it may surprise you how your awareness has the capacity to embrace many seemingly contradictory ideas and impressions without conflict.

You may encounter open-dimensionality, for example, when all of a sudden you see the ridiculousness of your own self-concern and burst into laughter, or when you see the irony of a painful situation and it reminds you that life is many things. Laughter brings levity and perspective to the most painful aspects of being human, such as racism, poverty, and death. Open-dimensionality reveals itself in those moments when we are unsure whether we should laugh or cry.

The notion of open-dimensionality challenges the assumption many of us have that the quality of openness is vague, directionless, and impractical. But is that how you really experience it? When you loosen the grip of your rigid sense of justice, the mind becomes agile, gains perspective, and reveals an acuity that finds inventive and intelligent ways to respond to life. Most importantly, your ability to see the open-dimensionality of things provides you with the basis from which to respond rather than react. It brings you out of delusion into seeing things as an illusion, whereby you can perceive the world with accuracy—meaning you don't have to make a mess.

Now that the delusion around your roommate has abated, you can begin to see how these problems you face present you with the creative aspect of being alive. Perhaps now that your impulses no longer run the show, you see new ways to navigate this situation.

Your roommate hands you that cup of coffee . . .

2

Investigating Things

The moment you begin to question that things may not be as they seem, the whole structure of your delusion begins to fall apart.

—Aryadeva

When you begin to understand the mechanics of delusion, you gain access to a powerful choice: Do you go along with the impulse to accept everything you see as real? Or do you feel ready to explore the possibility that things are not limited to your thoughts about them? This is a key decision. At first it may seem obvious: "The choice to see through delusion, please!" But that choice may not be as easy to make as you think. Most of us hold dearly to our truths, even if it hurts. When overwhelmed by disturbing thoughts and emotions, it can feel like you have little or no control, as if there were a biological mandate to react. Most likely, you have been burned again and again by reactive impulses, yet you find yourself doing the same things over and over. While you may desperately want to change, what about all these habits?

I bring this all up because, yes, in theory, you do have a choice. But the ability to actively seize this choice is something you will have to cultivate. Most of us are not habituated to staying open. We don't understand the nature of our thoughts and emotions. It takes some investigative wisdom to turn the tides of reactive mind.

My teacher once told me that the best he could ever do for anyone is to get them to self-reflect: to look at one's own mind and experience openly, free of judgment. Most of us are not accustomed to looking at the mind in a direct and simple way. Like so many others, you might think that honest self-reflection entails facing the scary things you generally try to avoid; and often your attempt at facing things results in an uncomfortable affirmation: "Wow, I'm pretty neurotic."

OK, but then what? You might think now is the time to put your story aside and turn to meditation. But while meditating you get even more overwhelmed by the rich energy of your thoughts, perceptions, and emotions. What do you do with it all? You wonder if it is even possible to enjoy the activity of your mind—all that stuff that constitutes your life.

In the next few sections I will introduce you to some ancient Buddhist instructions on how to look at experience with curiosity and openness, guided by an underlying respect for the natural expression of pratityasamutpada. The investigative path associated with the insight of pratityasamutpada, traditionally referred to in Sanskrit as Madhyamaka, or the Middle Way path, provides a way of exploring experience without getting overwhelmed by appearances. As we discussed in chapter 1, it is through misapprehending any experience as having intrinsic characteristics that we manifest delusion. But when you turn your focus to the nature of open-dimensionality, your ability to see beyond appearances becomes possible.

How does one begin? First of all, it is imperative to approach your investigation with a humble and open attitude. Imagine the quality of mind evoked by looking at something you have never seen before under a microscope or gazing out at the stars through a telescope for the first time. You can look at all of your experience with the same sense of awe. In fact, you will find some similarities between scientific exploration and your investigation here. Both rely on direct observation. The difference is that where scientists often do their best to silence the perceiver in their quest for objectivity, here you will explore the nature of knowing and its relationship to what you perceive. After all, you can't truly remove cognition from any inquiry. Because of this, the way in which one looks or investigates is of the utmost importance.

In the Buddhist approach we don't begin with a hypothesis or an experimental design. The instructions themselves won't dictate what you should or shouldn't see, feel, or think. That is for you to discover. In fact, the teachings encourage us to not attribute any truth or meaning whatsoever to experience. They do not aim at affirming, solving, or disproving anything. That would impede your ability to perceive things in a fresh and direct way. Instead, the objective is to poise your mind for what I call a *full* experience—that is, when you look directly at the natural expression of whatever arises without trying to capture, reject, or figure out what it is or is not.

The neuroscientist Francisco Varela called this kind of direct investigation "first-person science." He was intrigued by the ancient methodology of the Buddha. He understood that through including awareness in the investigation one could acquire more information about consciousness and experience than all the collected theories that science, psychology, or philosophy have ever come up with.

Before we move on, I want to clarify what I mean when I use the term *experience*. Experience here refers to that which comes before your awareness or, in this case, that which you bring into focus as the object of your investigation. As we apply the methods in the following chapters, we will deliberately bring the mind to bear on certain objects of experience, which might be material (such as a person or inanimate object) or might be a moment of consciousness (such as an emotion, a sensory perception, or a thought). Whatever comes before your awareness you can examine. You can even bring your attention to the knower or to knowing itself.

When considering the object of our consciousness, you may think of an inner experience as that which lies within the boundaries of your body. This is where most people assume their awareness resides. Yet you may also find that when you sit quietly and observe these inner experiences, they often seem to come at you from the outside.

In addition, those things that you consider to reside outside the boundaries of you cannot be separated from your perceptions of them. So while it may seem, at times, as though these investigations are solely an inward-facing exploration, as you observe your experience you may find that the lines between inside and outside are not so clear. What is inside? What is outside? It's hard to say.

What we call experience is truly a playful exchange of our inner and outer worlds. There is no problem with experience, in and of itself. The problem comes when the appearance of things outshines their nature and we begin to react. To release the mind from this very confusion constitutes the sole purpose of Middle Way investigations.

In this chapter, we will use our own physical body as the focal point or basis for our first investigation. We rarely give ourselves a chance to notice or respectfully observe the rich expression of our physical body, although we have all kinds of judgments or ideas about it. The actual presence of my body, or a body, as a singular and clearly delineated thing may not exist as you may assume it does. When you bring open awareness to the experience of the body, you will find an infinite universe rich with information. And you will notice that looking at your body requires the participation of your entire being.

(You can listen to an audio version of the following meditation and of the others in this book at www.shambhala.com/logicoffaithmeditations.)

Find a comfortable and natural sitting position so that you are relaxed yet attentive. The meaning of the term *relax* here refers to quieting the habit of continually blocking unwanted experiences or chasing after preferred ones.

Begin by bringing your awareness to the top of your head and slowly moving it down your body. It may be that wherever you place your awareness, it comes alive with sensation. If your body feels sleepy or dull, notice that dullness itself has its own sensation. (Otherwise, how would you identify and label it *dull*?)

Please do not judge what you encounter. See the dullness, or any other sensation or perception, as a natural and lively expression of mind and experience.

You may notice that observing your body also involves looking and seeing. You may not be looking with your eyes. Your eyes may be closed. But images express themselves in your mind's eye. You may have a visual image of energy moving in parts of your body, or you may picture certain parts of your body as you deliberately move your awareness from one area to another.

As you proceed, thoughts will arise, and there is no need to try to block them. They won't go away, in any case. Thoughts too are the natural expression of dependent arising. The thinking mind can still operate without you having to close down around conclusions—it has the ability to simply witness and navigate the flow of events that arise and dissipate. You can enjoy the moving and dynamic expression of language and concepts, which can be as fluid as everything you take in through your senses. And if you find yourself evaluating experience or getting lost in reifying labels, bring your focus back to the object of investigation, the body. Furthermore, take a moment to appreciate how your ability to discern brought you right back on track.

Continue to let any physical sensations reveal themselves to your awareness. At times experiment by deliberately bringing your attention to certain areas of your body. At other times, strong physical sensations will call your attention, like a cramp in your neck or perhaps your foot has fallen asleep and is starting to wake up and tingle or pulsate. Notice how sensations are not stuck in their place, how the moment you observe them and try to locate or describe them, they dissipate.

We have labels for the body as a whole, such as *me* or *I*, and we have terms for its composite parts, such as *bones, muscles, blood, sinew, limbs, head,* and *feet.* But that is not how we perceive the body when we bring an open, observant mind to our experience of it. Notice how the body and its parts are energetic, spacious, alive, and impossible to pin down.

I want to acknowledge that, at times, the body can feel like a receptacle for pain. But by placing your awareness on it, over time, you will find that your body is a source of wonder. If you tenderly turn your attention toward your body, it will come to life in unexpected ways. Even dullness, agitation, and congested or painful areas open up into less rigid and solid experiences. It is not that investigating the body protects you from feeling what you don't want to feel, but it will make you less resistant and more curious about the experiences you ordinarily contract around. This will allow your energy to flow and become less restricted. In this way the body can provide you with valuable information about the nature of nature of things, about your mind, and about being human. You may discover that what you call the body is an amazing universe unto itself and appreciate it as never before.

You can make your investigation as long or short as you wish. Sometimes your session will reach a natural ending, when you feel resolved and ready to go about your day. But do take a moment first to observe the open and humble qualities of investigative mind, and then try to bring this same spirit of curiosity out into your world.

The reason for investigating any experience, in the way we have just done, is to see that things do not exist as they appear. To look directly at the body, for instance, moves us out of vague assumptions into a direct relationship with the nature of pratityasamutpada. When we see beyond our coarse interpretations, we discover the less tangible and magical situation in which we actually live.

To understand what I mean by less tangible and magical, let's take another example, the notion of here. Here is different for everyone. Your here may be my there. And even when here is close enough for both of us to call it here, yours may be a little too close for me. Or it may be a little too far. Here is something intuitive and personal we all experience differently at different times with different people and things. We all agree upon what here means, but when we look for a here, we will see that it is only an idea—a vague approximation—of a place that we can't exactly point to. And yet, if you come here we can have an exchange, a conversation, or I can hand you something—maybe a gift. Here generally works quite well, even though you will never find a true here if you look directly. We all accept the illusion of here, but most of us have never questioned it.

In the same way that here is simply a vague approximation of a thing that functions well in the context of relative spatial agreements, the body too is a label for a congruence of lively experiences, which upon investigation can't be found. The point of investigation is not to simply reach a conclusive truth, which would become yet another reifying concept. Rather, the aim is to release your entire being from the misunderstanding that you are separate from the nature of mutual causality

LOOSENING PRACTICE

The intention [of analytical investigation] is not to refute sight, sound, or knowing. Our aim is to reverse the cause of suffering, clinging to things as real.

—Shantideva, *The Way of the Bodhisattva*

Unfortunately, the formal English term for investigating the nature of mind and experience in the context of pratityasamutpada is *analytical meditation*. I consider this unfortunate only because it's a term that often turns people off. How does it sound to you? You may enjoy analyzing things, as some people do. But you also may think that analytical meditation sounds about as inviting as dental work. You may have trouble understanding the connection between spirituality and analysis. Perhaps you came to the spiritual path to get away from concepts, and you prefer to take an intuitive or feeling approach to things.

To analyze a thing or idea generally means to methodically take it apart and scrutinize it. The process of taking things apart makes some people feel disembodied or disconnected—there can be a coldness to it, as if by analyzing things you are reducing the world you experience to dust. At other times, analysis just makes things more complicated and challenging to understand, like finding too many options while doing an Internet search. You start off with one idea and end up with way too many theories, too much information, too many maybes, worries, and too much stuff.

If you look up the etymology of the word *analysis*, it may surprise you to learn that it comes from the ancient Greek roots, *ana*, which means "to break up," and *lysis*, which means "to loosen." This definition fits perfectly with the purpose of analytical meditation, which is to break up and loosen your assumptions about things. Through analysis you move away from a coarser world of abstract ideas into a more direct relationship with what is actually going on.

Any time you break open or analyze something—even a word, the word *analysis*, for instance—something valuable will come out of it. If you place your attention on anything—be it an idea or a moment of anger or despair—your attentive analysis of it will reveal all kinds of surprises. New language and ideas will emerge—maybe even poetry. It is not that any one of these new expressions then becomes the be-all and end-all, the ultimate right idea or the correct usage of a term. You will never solve the mysteries of the universe. But you will open the door for more life to emerge, and, in turn, you can better appreciate the process of staying open and engaged, as though you were in the mode of listening intently to a fascinating interview, as in the example I mentioned earlier.

When engaging in analytical meditation, it is critical that you relate ideas to your own direct experience, rather than simply accepting things on hearsay. For instance, if someone tells you that everything arises interdependently, and you think, "Cool, that makes sense," you'll be left only with intellectual information that runs parallel to your experience, never deeply penetrating it and never releasing the confidence that comes only from seeing for yourself.

I hope I've made clear the spirit of this approach and that the term *analytical meditation* now makes sense to you. You are loosening this sense of realness, which helps you see the illusory nature of things, hence the term *analytical*. In doing this you are cultivating a different way of looking and knowing that perceives the nature of interdependence and open-dimensionality. When allowing your awareness to remain engaged and open, without succumbing to the need to affirm or deny experience, you can easily bear witness to the natural activity of mind. The technique of keeping the mind open refers to the meditative aspect of analytical meditation.

In Buddhist texts you find a Sanskrit term that describes the aspect of mind you depend on to intelligently engage experience, *prajna*. The most common etymological gloss for the term *prajna* (pronounced praj-nya) defines *pra* as "accurate" and *jna* as "awareness," "knowing," or "discernment." You could say that prajna accurately perceives things without impediment. For this reason it is used in the Buddhist teachings to mean insight into the nature of how things truly are.

You already have an intimate relationship with prajna. In the broadest sense, prajna serves as the guiding force you use to bring your actions together with your intentions. You rely on prajna while making simple choices at the grocery store or when choosing where you want to send your children to school. And you depend upon prajna in your longing for happiness and meaning. For instance, when you get distracted, when you daydream, or when you get lost in the proliferation of thoughts and disturbing emotions, when you stray from your intention, prajna brings you back on track. You find the wherewithal to pause and choose a more skillful, less reactive course of action, as in the roommate scenario earlier. Without the interference of prajna, you would probably be throwing your roommate's clothes out the window at this very moment. But something stopped you. That's prajna. Prajna can hold you in the boundary of your greater intentions and prevent you from making a mess.

As we have discussed, prajna, or discernment, cannot capture truth, but it can serve as the insight that will guide you if you pay attention. It is what we rely on to explore the mechanics of falling in and out of grace. If you have your sights set on moving out of delusion and into sane relationship with your world, bring prajna to the path of liberation.

Up until this point in the book, we have been exploring interdependence as the nature of all experience. In the next three sections I will present you with three analytical methods that will support your understanding of dependent arising. But first I want to give you some background.

Following the Buddha, the many great meditation masters who came after him (such masters as Nagarjuna, Chandrakirti, Kamalashila, Shantarakshita, and Shantideva, to mention only a few) taught creative and powerful methods for seeing through the illusion of an independent reality. But all of their systems stem from the Buddha's teachings on interdependence and pivot on the same basic question: Can you find anything—whether animate, inanimate, made of matter, or immaterial—that exists outside the great nature of interdependence?

Together we will engage three investigations pertaining to this question: We will first look for anything that is singular, meaning something that is not composed of parts. Then we will try to locate something that is permanent, in other words, something that is always so and doesn't change. And last of all, we will search for something that is independent, something that does not arise based on causes and conditions and that is not influenced by other elements.

Analytical meditation—that is, the process of searching for a real thing—is essentially an unbrainwashing process. Kongtrul Rinpoche told me that when, as a young monk, he first started to investigate the realness of things, he would drape his monk's shawl, or *zen*, around his head to create an undistracted cave-like atmosphere. He would spend hours trying to find anything that existed outside the nature of relationship, sometimes using the conceptual mind, sometimes focusing directly on perception and sensation. To look at the interdependent nature of things in a precise way doesn't mean you have to get hypervigilant, self-focused, and neurotic. If you adopt a humble and childlike curiosity, the nature of interdependence will surprise, charm, and delight you. In fact, you may even fall in love with your mind and its world.

As we look together for anything that is permanent, singular, and autonomous, please probe with a little fierceness. You can fuel that fierceness with devotion to the insight of pratityasamutpada or recall an experience of grace, in order to inspire you. But the most important thing to remember, as you proceed through this investigation, is to have a humble mind, open to learning. If you do, who knows what you will discover? It may be that you do find an autonomous thing—something that has an independent nature. You may find something that never changes or is not made of parts and that exists outside the nature of pratityasamutpada. Maybe you will find a truth that all the great masters of this tradition have not yet found. You need to be open to this. And if you do find such a thing, you should write your own book. I will definitely read it, and others will undoubtedly read it too.

If you think about it, everyone is looking for objective truths. Scientists continuously search for a partless particle—a fundamental force or component of mass that produces all matter and that can't be further broken. Do you suppose there is such a thing that has no parts and exists objectively from its own side? Philosophers have devised theories around the meaning of life, the human condition, and the causes of suffering. Do you suppose any single one of them is true? Spiritual seekers have pursued an ontological presence or primal force responsible for the creation of the universe. Can they find anything that is intrinsically true, that everyone can agree on?

Throughout history, no one has ever found an intrinsic truth. And why is this? It is because everything leans. Given that this is the case, chances are you won't find a definitive truth either. Yet such a thing is worth looking for, because as you search for a real thing, chances are you will encounter not finding—and not finding will be your source of liberating insight.

DON'T MAKE IT A THING!

It is not down in any map; true places never are.

—Herman Melville

For our first investigation we will search for something that has the quality of singularity—that is, for something that is not made of parts. You may wonder, "Why would anyone spend their precious time looking for something singular? What purpose would that serve?"

When we use language to describe the world, whether our thoughts, feelings, perceptions, or objects, we usually refer to them nominally as things: an iPhone, the sun, love, a moment of time, me, a surprise, a problem, an enemy, a hero, an atom, a reaction, or a moment of bliss, a circumstance. A thing, by definition, can only exist in one of two ways: it has to be singular or many. When we use terms like, *a forest, a herd of elk, a swarm of bees*, or *a mass of energy*, we are basically grouping a collection of singular things into one general thing. We do perceive and take in all these things through our senses in a nonconceptual way, but the moment we begin to cognize and assign labels to them, they always become either singular things or many things.

Such collections of experiences are known in the Buddhist tradition as aggregates, *skandhas* in Sanskrit and *pungpo* in Tibetan. In fact, Dzigar Kongtrul Rinpoche actually refers to my dense, lumpy cookies as pungpos. Yes, they are a bit hard to bite into, so you may assume they can't be broken, but I assure you, they are a compound of many healthy ingredients, like eggs, almond flour, and flax seeds.

To lump together and name things is not necessarily a problem. In fact, labels are useful. But the point here is to understand that the nature of things will always remain free of the constraints of the labels you assign them. Thoughts do not provide you with direct access to reality, rather with snapshots or impressions once removed from the world you encounter with your senses. They are like maps—abstract representations of a vast terrain of mutually caused expression.

Imagine you had a map of a hiking trail in the mountains. Upon arriving at the trailhead, you would not expect the map to bear any resemblance to the terrain itself. True, a map can show you how to navigate the trail. But unlike the one-dimensional design of your map, the actual trail you encounter would be a place animated and teeming with life. You would see birds, swarms of pesky mosquitos, rocks, prickly grasses, and wildflowers. You would discover shady places to rest, open vistas, and shortcuts. You would breathe in the scent of fresh pine and feel the breeze on your skin. A map is the description, not the described.

As you began to walk the territory the map is based on, you might also wonder if a tree could be thought of as a map. Isn't *tree* simply a label you apply to a collection of parts: the trunk, branches, pine needles, pinecones, and so forth? And if you isolate any single one of those parts, say, a cone, you find that it in itself is another grouping of parts: petals, seeds, pine nuts, and a core comprised of individual fibers. The *cone* would be revealed as a map or designation placed upon yet another collection of specific elements.

Do you see where this is going? You can continue to apply the same logic to the smallest particle available to the naked eye and then even to the atomic level and beyond. In fact, this all suggests that as long as you ascertain the presence of a thing you can analyze it. Whether a thing is large or small, material or conscious, makes no difference. It is the notion of thingness—which stems from seeing things as whole, complete, or inviolably singular—that we are questioning here.

It may interest you to note that in ancient Greece the word *atom* used to refer to something that could not be broken or cut—something that resisted analysis. There has been a lot of scientific exploration since then. Atoms are no longer seen as unbreakable. In fact entire universes of phenomenal surprises have burst from the confines of their so-called unbreakable nature. During the 1950s and '60s physicists discovered so many particles in scattering experiments—quarks, strings, leptons, gluons—that they began to refer to that period of exploration as the time of the "particle zoo."

The point here is that as long as you can locate a singular object—as minute or subtle as it might be—you can break it down into parts. As long as you ascribe thingness to any occurrence, object, or perception—even if it is just a theory—it will be susceptible to analysis.

Why is it important to investigate things? Why did all the great Indian Buddhist scholars and meditators in this tradition, whose sole interest in life focused on seeing through delusion, think this was so important? What relevance does questioning singularity or thingness have to do with your life? Let's bring this question to a personal investigation.

To begin with, sit in a comfortable position, and spend as much time as you need to settle the mind by focusing on your breath. When you feel ready, try to identify something in your life that challenges you, something you would rather not experience. When choosing your thing—which will serve as the object of your investigation—try to avoid tackling something that might stir you up too much. Please view this as a gentle experiment. Just dip your toe in at first.

You may choose to examine a physical discomfort (the underlying tightness, worry, or stress that seems to follow you around all day) or a feeling of darkness, repulsion, self-doubt, or mild depression. Or you may want to single out a relationship conflict or a situation you are presently working with. When you select your object of investigation, notice how just in isolating one aspect of your experience and labeling it, it becomes a singular thing, just like a map.

That you can single out or map experiences is crucial to your investigation and an expression of prajna, your natural ability to discern. Labels and thoughts are powerful tools that allow you to bring that which is general and vague into the light of your awareness. We need maps to explore. Now that you have a map, you can venture into the actual terrain of this thing to see what awaits you.

Before we continue, I want to remind you that *analysis* means "to loosen." The purpose of the practice, in this case, is to loosen or crack open assumptions you have regarding the singularity or thingness of your object by observing its parts or aspects. In other words, you will use the power of discernment, or prajna, to move out of abstract notions into a more direct relationship with experience. Be clear: you are not searching for a truth about your object, nor are you looking for its cause. Keep an open and curious mind. This will protect you from getting lost in the habit of reaching conclusions or thinking you know what this thing is.

You probably identify strongly with your thing. You may see yourself as "the one with the physical pain" or identify with mysterious patterns of discomfort or depression, or you might blame something external as the cause of your unhappiness. Your focus may drift to the past, or your attention might leap ahead to proliferating fantasies you have about the future. Just notice this, and bring the mind back to the investigation. You can tend to the practicalities of life's demands later if you have to. For now, commit a little bit of time to looking at your thing in a new way. It may influence the way you respond to the circumstance afterward.

As you explore the landscape of your thing, can you identify a presence, mood, or atmosphere? How would you describe it? You may encounter waves of moving or stuck energy, physical contraction, shortness of breath, unsettling emotions, heaviness, or wild discursive thoughts and judgments. Or you may be surprised to find moments of lightness, stillness, or many other unexpected things.

The philosopher of mind and language, Ludwig Wittgenstein, once said, "Only describe; don't explain." In that spirit we are not trying to define anything—we are not creating maps here but merely observing or describing the terrain.

Take as much time as you need on each piece of the investigation. If the mind wanders, come back to your body. Try scanning your body with your awareness, starting at the crown of your head, moving downward. Where do you feel the areas of concentrated energy? Do you find yourself fixating on uncomfortable sensations or attached to blissful ones? See if you can locate them as things. You might discover, in exploring them, a flurry of sensations. Can you single out one sensation and repeat the investigation? As you focus your attention on any one thing, new things will reveal themselves to you.

At this point we are going to shift our focus to the defining edges of things. Begin by identifying the different parts of your body: limbs, head, neck, and so on. Although you can, in a general way, identify and name these parts, see if you can pinpoint exactly where the shoulder meets the arm. Can you identify precisely where your forearm meets your hand? Can you locate exactly where your knee ends and your leg begins? Where does your head become your neck?

If the task of locating body parts seems too obvious to your gross conceptual mind to be of interest, remember that you are not asking the labeling mind to make these distinctions. You are going for a direct experience, unrestricted by labels and assumptions.

When you feel ready, take a moment to reflect on your discoveries. Did you find your singular thing? What did you encounter while walking its terrain? Could you find anything not composed of parts? If you found parts, were these parts singular or did they possess, in turn, more parts? Could you find one or many of anything? Do you suspect that is even possible?

You may have discovered that analysis penetrates the realness of your thing—opening you into an infinite world of interconnected relationships, freeing you from the confines of your truths. You may actually have less of an idea about what your thing is now than ever before. Yet if you avoid grasping for the truth, you won't feel the least bit confused. This is because seeing the interdependent nature of things simplifies your relationship to experience, making it less vague, less abstract, and less intimidating. To think you know the truth of a thing through its label is not an accurate assessment of its mode of being.

I'm sure you are familiar with the expression "Don't make it a thing!" Someone, witnessing you on the edge of losing it, might attempt to intervene by suggesting that you are reading too much meaning into a situation. "Don't make it a thing" can remind you that your story is congealing and getting in the way of your ability to see the dynamic and full energy of something that is not a definitive truth and can be perceived in various ways. This is not to say you shouldn't respond to whatever is happening. The wisdom here is simply "Don't assume you know what it is." Then let discernment guide you. I am certain you will be surprised at how very effective, clear, and appropriate you can be in that situation.

In particular, unwanted experiences we have in life tend to haunt us. We spend so much time bracing ourselves against them or doubting whether we can face their intensity. But when we look for these so-called scary or disturbing things, we find curiously that we cannot affirm them. They don't exist as singular, and they also don't exist as many. Well, how do they exist then? You may find yourself in uncharted territory here because while you can't affirm things, you can't deny them either!

To bear witness to this extraordinary observation requires a little humility and inquisitiveness. As you look directly at singular things you will see that everything just keeps opening and opening, and you can enjoy that. That is the practice.

SEARCHING FOR A PERMANENT OR IMPERMANENT SELF

One of the most misleading representational techniques in our language is the use of the word "I."

—Ludwig Wittgenstein

Can you locate anything in this universe that is not subject to change? Seasons turn; the moon waxes and wanes; our favorite television series come and go, as do trends in fashion and technology. Change becomes vividly apparent as we watch our children mature, our parents grow old, and our friends and neighbors move away. Even on a cellular level our bodies are in a constant state of flux. Find a photograph of yourself when you were a toddler. As you gaze at your image, you may feel nostalgic for your youth or the relief of maturity. But mostly, looking back will remind you of what you already know: that the only constant in life is change.

However, despite our recognition of change, we still hold tightly to permanence in some deep and subtle ways. You most likely assume, for instance, that there is a continuous self that does all this changing. I was there as a shy little girl, clinging to my mom's skirt the first day of nursery school. I am an adult now, looking at my own young child. This "I" has been the constant witness to my entire life, as far back as I can remember. I also identify with reoccurring patterns and preferences as being me. For instance, I have always loved horses, disliked spinach, and (I have often been told) been impossibly stubborn. This has been me as far back as I can remember. At other times I connect my identity to isolated events, for instance, the I that got jilted twenty years ago may still be around narrating and reaffirming her story.

Yes, I-you-we have all changed over the years, but something seems to have carried over from past to present. You probably wouldn't say you are the same person you were as a child but neither would you say that you are completely different. You have an intimate connection to that animated little person in the photo through memory, family relationships, behavioral patterns, and recognizable physical features. There appears to be a physical and conscious thread that holds it all together.

In the Middle Way tradition, to question the continuum of a permanent self is not a denial of who you are as a fully functional, living, breathing human being with a unique history. Rather its purpose is to address the question "What continues?" Because when you begin to look for this I, you may find its presence ambiguous at best. You may also find it curious that you have such a vague relationship with the thing you are most intimate with, this self you hold so dear. Let's make this permanent self the object of our next investigation.

Sit quietly in a comfortable position, breathe naturally, and let your mind settle. You can keep your eyes either open or closed. When you feel ready, ask yourself, "Where is the self?" At first, you may feel a bit flustered—even dizzied—by this question because your sense of self is both everywhere and nowhere at the same time. It is perfectly OK to feel perplexed. This is a sign that the wisdom of the question is pushing at your unexamined assumptions. This experience, in and of itself, is a crucial first step in the examination.

At the same time, you will need to ground yourself in the investigation. An effective way to do this is to bring your attention to your body. After all, it is the body we most strongly associate with the self. Chances are you frequently say such things as "I am strong" or "I feel sleepy." So look into the physical body, and see if you can find a consistent or permanent self in the body.

You might begin by using the top of your head as the initial focal point and proceed by bringing your awareness slowly down your face, neck, limbs, and so on. Search your entire body for an unchanging self by asking, "Is the self in my head . . . my eyes . . . my limbs . . . my heart?" There may be areas where you feel strong sensation; search these areas for a permanent, continuous self.

When you have looked and feel certain that the self cannot be found in the various parts of the body, see if you can find a self in the body as a whole, as a sum of its parts. In looking for the self in the entirety of the body, first ask yourself if you can locate this whole body. Try to visualize your entire body at once, and see if you can find a consistent image that doesn't change. See if you can feel your body as a whole, unchanging thing. See if you can even think of or perceive the body as a whole, permanent, or unchanging entity. If your body and your perceptions of it were static, it would be simple to identify its wholeness. But you might find that impossible. Finally, I think you will have to ask yourself how a consistent entity, the self, could be equated with the dynamic and elusive force, the body.

As you explore your body, it probably won't take long for you to recognize that the way you refer to the self is inconsistent and shifty. Sometimes you equate the self with the body, but other times you refer to it as the owner of the body. After all, when you say, "My foot is asleep" or "I have an itch," you are referring to the self as the proprietor of the body and its sensations, while earlier you identified it *as* the body. See if you can find this elusive self that governs the body.

Ask the question: Does the self, as the proprietor of the body, reside within or outside the perimeters of its form? If self abides outside the boundaries of my body, where or what is it? If it resides within the body, in which part does it settle? Try to find this permanent entity—the proprietor of the body—that doesn't change. Probe deeply and directly; don't give this investigation over to the labeling mind.

Remember: The purpose of this investigation is to exhaust some deeply rooted, unexamined assumptions you have about the true mode of existence of a continuous and permanent self. Only through looking and not finding will you ever feel confident about its actual mode of being.

When or if you feel convinced that you can't find a consistent self in connection to the body, you may insist that although the self eludes you, something must be there; you can feel it.

Look at the experiences that arise in your awareness—all that wanting, needing, all the joys, fears, and sorrows. Who is behind all this pulling the strings in its attempt to cherish, maintain, and protect its existence? Try to find the one who feels, who aspires, or who dreads. Can you find a permanent self amid this constant quest for survival?

If this permanent self continues to elude you, you may conclude, "OK, maybe the self is not an actual thing, but there certainly is some kind of atmospheric presence that I can't ignore." You may describe it as a continuous din of white noise in the background like your neighbor's radio, an omnipresent narrator who seems to shadow you day and night evaluating your performance, the advocate who turns up in times of need to console you, or your conscience. Yes, someone or something seems to preside somewhere—but where exactly can you find it?

It may finally occur to you that the one doing the searching is the self. Ask yourself which self is true: the one doing the searching or the one being searched for? Is self the seer or the seen? Is it the subject or the object? It may be hard to distinguish the two. After all, the moment you begin to look at the subject, it becomes the object of another moment of subjective awareness.

You may conclude then that the permanent self must be a neutral observer—awareness itself—that takes in and records information, like a camera in a bank. But how can awareness ever be neutral or permanent? Have you ever experienced a conscious moment that was not influenced by what it observed? Doesn't knowing change in dependence upon its object? Can you see, hear, touch, or smell without an object of perception? What would it be like if your awareness—that which you now assume to be the self—remained uninfluenced by its changing world? How could such a self experience anything?

Having located many faces of the self, perhaps you have concluded that self must exist in *all* of them, like an actor who keeps changing costumes. But if the self changes from advocate to judge to the spokesperson for your conscience, then shifts to various parts of your body, and back and forth from being a subject and an object, can you call it a permanent or continuous entity? What part of this *impermanent* self can you identify as permanent or continuous?

You may be asking yourself a question just about now: "How, if there is nothing permanent that continues, is there any cohesion to experience?" There must be some sort of central organizing principle that holds it all together. Otherwise, what would explain the sequence of you as a child growing into you as an adult or the linearity of an apple seed growing into an apple tree, not a banana tree or a rock? "Continuity," you may argue, "is an observable fact of nature."

But there is a contradiction buried deep within the notion of a continuum of impermanence—that there is something that retains its identity as it keeps changing. Hmmm. This question concerning linearity requires a deep and subtle investigation of impermanence.

One of the main ways we attempt to comprehend and measure the change we see around us is by looking at it through the framework of time. Like most people, you probably organize your day—and life— into a strand of incremental units: seconds, minutes, hours, years, and so on. Time is an elegant tool for punctuality, for measuring progress on a project, and for understanding history. But time is no more than a consensual agreement that helps us identify and navigate change.

Tom O'Brian, America's official timekeeper at the National Institute of Standards and Technology in Boulder, Colorado, said once on National Public Radio: "My own personal opinion is that time is a human construct . . . [a way to] put some order in this very fascinating and complex universe around us."[1] Tom's job is to keep the clock ticking at an accurate pace. This is not an easy task considering that—due to many interdependent factors, such as gravity and altitude—the movement of a clock's hand doesn't move at the same rate everywhere in the universe.

In order to examine the assumption that life arises in discrete moments, I would like to introduce you to an investigation into the nature of time.

Begin by finding a comfortable position, and then turn your focus toward the notion of time to see if it has any basis in the reality you directly perceive. Begin by trying to locate a present moment. You may discover that the instant you even conceive of the present, it has already dissolved. You could almost say that the present is now the future, yet it is always just a step ahead of you.

People often talk about living in the present, but can you *find* a present moment? If such a thing could be found, it would, by definition, have to have duration to distinguish it from the past and future. How long does it endure? As long as the tick of a clock? See if what you call the present moment is not a compound of many moments. Can you point to the instant when the past becomes the present or the present becomes the future? As long as there is a unit of time—a disparate moment—you can further divide it into past, present, and future.

Spend some time on this investigation. Probe deeply using your ability to directly observe things. Don't hand this inquiry over to the mind that draws artificial boundaries around experience, such as moments of time. Search for one discrete moment that is not made of smaller moments. See if you can capture time. See if experience actually arises in discrete units.

Change is an aspect of what you refer to as continuum. In a coarse way, you see things arise in sequential moments: past, present, and future. But when you look directly at experience, do you ever actually see the moment that one thing changes into another thing?

Think of drawing a line on the surface of a still lake. Although you see a line, you will never be able to locate the occurrence of its arising or its dissolution into the water. Arising and dissolving seem to happen simultaneously—or perhaps not at all. But that doesn't mean you can't see the line. It's just that although the line reveals itself to you vividly, you will never find a trace of its continuum or be able to locate its beginning, middle, or end.

In order to explore this more directly, let's do another investigation.

Again, find a comfortable position, and when you are ready, ask yourself if you can pinpoint the instant night becomes the dawn. You may at first think that dawn arises when you spot the glow of light on the horizon or when you first see the lines appear on the palm of your hand. But when you look closely, can you precisely point to when that dawning took place—as an actual occurrence? Can you accurately single out a sunset moment? Can you point out the true edge of twilight or night? Do you see it happen even as you sit on your porch with your full attention focused upward toward the sky?

And if you are a parent, ask yourself this: Do you remember the instant your infant became a toddler? A child? A teenager? When parents watch their child do something new, they proudly exclaim, "Now he's a man!" But as a direct experience, who can truly say when manhood occurred? Yes, the various phases of our lives are distinct, yet we never actually change from one singular or permanent thing into another. Just look in the mirror and try asking yourself, "At what point did I get old?"

We often use the phrase "the time of death," but it is not clear when we actually die. We cannot determine the exact moment of death because it resembles night changing to dawn or the sound of a bell fading away. We cannot identify the particular moment something is born or, conversely, the moment it falls into extinction. But on a coarser level, birth and death most certainly seem to occur.

You can understand through all of these examples that when you look directly at experience, you will not find any substantial thing arising, staying, or dissolving. Things are unfindable, yet they express themselves in a continuous succession nonetheless. To see the illusory nature of things frees us from clinging to thingness.

The shift from seeing things as impermanent to seeing their unborn or unfindable nature is not only a philosophical shift. Experientially, it moves us from the tender heart of sadness (where one grapples with the impermanence of old age, sickness, and death) to a sense of awe, magic, and fearlessness. This is the liberation that characterizes the specific insight of the Middle Way path.

You have looked for a permanent self in the body and in the objects of the senses. And you have looked for self as the knower of experience, as subjective mind. I have a hunch you didn't find a permanent continuous self in residence. However, it frequently happens that one's conceptual mind finds itself at odds with its own discovery, and one begins to doubt one's own direct experience. It is common for a new investigator to interpret not finding as a negation of experience, even though the point of the investigation is to liberate the mind from the conceptual constraints of is and is not, affirmation and denial.

The disconnect that often arises between direct experience and conceptual understanding comes up almost every time I introduce this investigation of self to a gathering of people. At least one person in the group will get frustrated, protesting, "How can you say there is no self?" I always find it humorous because I take great care *not* to assert that there is *no* self. I simply ask people to look for one—that's it.

Just in case you find yourself at such a juncture and feel a bit unsure at this point in your process, I want to reassure you that all is well. It is only a matter of time before a motivated investigator breaks through the constraints of her or his assumptions, but when it happens, it is really exciting.

Remember: Here we are not looking through the lens of habitual mind and its assumptions. We are simply trying something new. No need to get too philosophical about it. Let yourself feel the blessings of the inquiry: enjoy your open and inquisitive mind.

FROM SCRATCH: INVESTIGATING AUTONOMY

I am not contained between my hat and boots.

—Walt Whitman

In this section let's see whether we can find anything that doesn't lean. We will be looking for something that stands alone, something that isn't influenced by other elements or dependent upon causes and conditions. Do you think you can find such a thing?

In the 1960s and '70s the cosmologist and astronomer Carl Sagan challenged the notion of autonomy with a statement: "If you wish to make an apple pie from scratch, you must first invent the universe."

In the good old days everyone had time to make pies from scratch. No one had invented piecrust mixes (yet). Then in the 1930s and '40s some industrious person started marketing boxes of premixed piecrust ingredients, and in the 1950s cultural icon Betty Crocker made the product even more prevalent. Her packaged ingredients only required the addition of water and oil—sometimes eggs. Thanks to Betty, we now have a choice: we can save the time it takes to measure ingredients and crack eggs, or we can go at it the old-fashioned way and start from scratch.

But even if you do go the old-fashioned route, does that extra bit of work it takes to mix individual ingredients together constitute baking a pie from scratch? In your attempt to make a pie from scratch, where would you begin? You might learn to farm. You then would have to buy some land, set up an irrigation system, acquire some heavy machinery (or at least a draft horse and plow), and collect some seeds. You may feel satisfied that if you were to plant seeds, harvest, thresh, and grind the wheat into the flour with which to make your piecrust, you would have made an apple pie from scratch. But in fact, each individual seed has an origin—each one came from generations of wheat plants. You can never know the story of each individual seed; you can only infer that at some point in time someone discovered a wheat plant and recognized its potential.

According to historians, wheat originated in the Levant region of the Near East, along the Fertile Crescent. They have recently narrowed the location down to Turkey, where wheat dates as far back as 7,500 B.C.E. As far as we know, the survival of wheat has always relied upon sunshine, water, carbon dioxide, and nutrient-rich soil. Wheat required farmers, landowners, and workers to process it into flour. I'm sure there were all kinds of politics around the economics and distribution of wheat, as there are now.

You could focus your attention on nothing but the origin of wheat for eternity and never exhaust the topic. That's because in looking at the interconnectedness of anything, you will find endless stories, information, challenges, and adventures, which will again open into other stories, and so on. You will never reach definitive conclusions about this thing you call wheat. Like all things, its nature is boundless and free of the constraints of your designating labels.

And we haven't even gotten to the apples yet.

Carl Sagan's quote once inspired me to make an apple pie. It was August, my tree was heavy with apples, my dad's birthday was around the corner, and he loves apple pie. Lucky for me, my dear friend Peggy Markel, who takes people on exotic cooking tours in places like Morocco, Italy, and India, paid me a visit. The evening before her arrival I had planned on harvesting the apples from my tree. But that night a bear ravaged them all with the exception of one little apple, which fearfully clung to the top of the only branch the bear hadn't torn away from the tree's trunk. There is a lot contingent upon making an apple pie, and sometimes the universe seems to conspire against you! Instead of reading too much into it though, I just went to town and bought a bag of local apples.

Making a good apple pie requires a lot of experimentation. Peggy and I played with kneading the dough by hand versus putting it all in a food processor. We tried adding more or less water to get the best consistency. We had to adjust the oven temperature for high altitude. And there are numerous styles of apple pies to choose from—rustic, traditional, the kind with a lattice upper crust, apple crumble, and tarte tatin, just to name a few. Each has its own history and place of origin, and we tried many variations, employing most of my kitchen tools, pie pans, and ingredients. Peggy, it turns out, is tireless when it comes to the science of pie making, and we worked through every possibility.

At the end of the day, I felt proud, in particular, of our most traditional creation, which we decorated with leaves shaped of dough. I felt as if we had really accomplished something—but only for a moment. Sagan's words came back to me to put a halt to my bravado, reminding me that I couldn't possibly be the sole cause of this pie. This pie was not the product of one person's pie-making inspiration—one recipe, one list of ingredients, or one baker to execute it. The creation of this pie was not the result of a singular cause. It wasn't a linear process at all. In fact, it took full-on universal participation. I think this is Sagan's point: an apple pie is not a closed system but relies upon the cooperation of the entire universe.

At first glance, Carl Sagan's statement seems to challenge us to find where an apple pie ends and the world begins. But I suspect his intention was to get us to think about something that goes way beyond dessert. I think his words were meant to provoke us into exploring who we are in relationship to the universe. His statement shows us that who we are—the experiencer—and the world we perceive are not the same or separate, not one or two, but rather share a relationship of interdependence. You can apply the same analysis to your self. Where do you end and does your world begin?

Think about the origin of you. You may think of the story as a linear history. Your parents met, say, at their university. Think of all the causes and conditions that had to come together for that to happen! They could have gone to different schools. Or even if they attended the same school, what if their friends hadn't introduced them? Or having met, what if one of them wasn't impressed? Or what if one of them had a fatal accident just after they were married? And what if things hadn't panned out biologically? When you begin to look at conception, gestation, and the survival of a fetus in the womb, you enter into an entire universe of contingency. You will encounter the life of zygotes, dividing cells, and hormones. You will come to see that your existence hinged on a single and tenacious sperm's "decision" to turn right instead of left at the intersection of your mom's fallopian turnpikes. Then, if "he" made it to the egg, "she" had to deem him worthy of acceptance. After conception takes place the life of the fetus then relies on a billion other things to go right—but wow, here you are. What a miracle.

What are the causes and conditions that brought you to where you are, in this very moment? Use the prowess of your imagination—explore. Don't dismiss your imagination as invalid or untrue. Remember: All thoughts and memories are imaginary. Yet the way you understand your world has a potent effect on the direction your life takes and how you navigate it. Let yourself explore this fathomless self that has no boundary, no beginning or end—that keeps opening and opening into galaxies of experience.

When I think about the nature of pratityasamutpada, I am overcome with gratitude and awe. I might say that this aspect of my mind is what I cherish most—but it's not really an aspect of mind. It is what I experience when I am not confused about who I am in the larger scheme of things. When I feel connected to the infinite nature of interdependent expression, I call that grace.

Maybe you are beginning to catch on to how the practices of pratityasamutpada help you see beyond a mistaken notion of a singular, permanent, or autonomous me. This seeing through the self is something many people have contemplated. In fact, Einstein once said that what humans single out as a separate self is a kind of optical delusion of our consciousness.

The meteorologist Edward Lorenz, when exploring the interconnectedness of weather patterns, asked his famous question: "Does a butterfly fluttering its wings in Brazil set off a tornado in Texas?" Because everything leans, something as delicate as the wings of a butterfly has reverberating effects on everything that happens everywhere in the entire cosmos and beyond. So imagine what that means for you too.

The investigations of the Middle Way tradition make it clear that autonomy will never be an option. So don't waste your time trying to single yourself out of the bigger picture. You are not big, nor are you small. You are not important, nor are you insignificant. And you cannot be affirmed or denied. You are not the same as everything else, but neither are you separate. You are beyond the limitations of ordinary thinking, and you cannot be captured in thought.

So just in case you are still wondering, "But who am I then?" on behalf of the late Mr. Sagan I will respond in a way I think he would have agreed: "You are a part of the great nature of contingency, and everything you do matters."

EMPTINESS

Because the nature of everything is emptiness, it is possible to view our life the way we would view a movie. We can relax and enjoy the show.

—Dzigar Kongtrul Rinpoche, *It's Up to You*

I was in my early twenties when Kongtrul Rinpoche introduced me to the same three investigations we just undertook together here. As I began to practice them I struggled to reconcile these new ideas with some beliefs I had about how things are. My thinking mind and my experience had yet to come together. I kept asking my teacher how things could possibly appear and yet be unfindable at the same time. Things seemed real—after all I could point to them! He kept patiently pointing me back to the practice so that I would develop confidence based on my direct experience.

Sometimes he would give me a little something to chew on. I remember him once saying, "Lizzy, it's magic." Back then that statement didn't satisfy me at all. I would silently complain to myself: "What kind of explanation is that?" But I continued to probe because

I had to see for myself. And then, one day as I was driving my son to nursery school, in what seemed like an instant, something clicked. My conceptual mind caught up with the direct experience that resulted from my investigative persistence, and my world opened up in the most unexpected and spectacular way.

Of course, I'm not making the claim that after having that experience "I have arrived" and that appearances no longer seduce me or that I no longer get caught up in the realness of my daily concerns. I am a work in progress. But underneath it all I have a sense of what is actually going on—I am not completely fooled. At times when someone does something that stirs me up—as right as I try to convince myself that I am—underneath it all I have conviction that the way I see this person in the moment could not possibly capture the reality of who he or she truly is. I may experience fear, anger, or insecurity, but I know that the object of such emotions is naturally unrestricted by my projections and misunderstandings. This tempers my usual knee-jerk reaction to things. It gives me a powerful choice: I have the option to not take things at face value.

In those rare and precious moments of grace, when you can enjoy the open-dimensionality of things, you will feel emancipated from your fears and insecurities. You will find that your ability to not be right—to see the illusory nature of things—releases an unshakable confidence, clear seeing, and joy in you. This is not a conceptual confidence that you can yet again cling to as truth—it is a confidence that arises from directly observing your world continue to open and open, never for a moment settling into thingness.

The brilliance that comes from not shutting down around experience makes you less reactive and fearful, and more flexible, savvy, and loving. Those who have practiced the teachings throughout time have described their experience in this way.

Once, upon receiving teachings from Kongtrul Rinpoche on a particularly profound text, I confided to him that the more I studied the teachings of pratityasamutpada, the more they astonished me. As I continue to investigate and study them, I see that I have only skimmed the surface of their depths. And he replied, "Me too."

When I realized that he experienced them in the same way, I also came to realize that the arising of the qualities of awe and humility are an indication that the teachings have come to life in you. You should know that this practice leads to less knowing and more awe, which is really just a way of speaking about a deeper kind of wisdom. For me it has become clear that this place of awe is the place from which I want to live.

It might seem that having conviction in the unfindable nature of things would lead to a kind of indifference or immunity to suffering. But I would argue that this practice does not make you invulnerable to life, not at all. In fact, the opposite seems to be the case. The teachings and practices of pratityasamutpada broaden your capacity to include every aspect of life in your experience. Thus, to accept that you don't know things in a determinate way is not an admission of loss or defeat. The fact is that things have always been unfindable and illusory, so there's nothing to lose. But there is something to gain: you inherit the precious and extremely rare choice to either live in ignorance or to come alive with the liberating insight of pratityasamutpada.

Dzogchen Ponlop Rinpoche, a contemporary Tibetan Buddhist teacher who has widely contributed to the spread of pratityasamutpada wisdom in the West, once teased a group of students by saying, "If you want things to be real, don't analyze them!" That's true. You don't have to look into the nature of things. But the big question is why wouldn't you? Who would actively not want to pursue a life in accord with the fluid and magical—yes, *magical*—nature of things? Would you prefer to deceive yourself in order to avoid this magic instead?

The wisdom of pratityasamutpada came from a profound yet utterly simple realization. The Buddha described this insight in his famous declaration on the morning of his awakening, when he said, "This being, that becomes; from the arising of this, that arises; this not being, that becomes not; from the ceasing of this, that ceases."[2]

Even after some study, you could miss the nuance of his words. They may seem obvious. You observe the law of cause and effect on a coarse level and interpret it simply as things being in relationship with other things. But the Buddha cautioned us not to stop there. He described the realization of pratityasamutpada as "deep, subtle, hard to perceive, and requiring insight."[3] The fact that everything leans does more than just point us to the world of relationship. It leads us into a process of directly understanding that we will never find anything we can identify as either singular or many, either inherently permanent or impermanent, or either the same or separate from other things. In effect, we will never find these so-called things that are in relationship to other things.

The Buddha had a name for the unfindable nature of things. He called it "emptiness," or *shunyata*, in Sanskrit. *Emptiness* is a tough word for most people. It seems to dismiss the world of appearance outright. When people hear the word *emptiness*, they often associate it with nothingness, like a void or a black hole. When someone suggests to you that things are empty, you may feel like that person is inviting you to a party in an apartment located in a deserted and bleak part of town, where there is no heat, food, music, or wine. When introduced to the notion of emptiness, people often panic, get angry—even insulted—as if you are trying to take away their joie de vivre. They say, "I thought you told me that everything was in relationship! What do you mean there are no things?" I can sometimes literally watch the warmth drain from their investigation when the idea of emptiness is introduced.

But as my teacher did with me, I always remind them, "Don't worry; you won't lose your connection to relationship. No one can take the nature of interdependence away from you! It's impossible." You can't take the colors or arc away from a rainbow. Apple seeds will always produce apple trees. At the same time, can you deny that these things that arise dependent upon other things can't be found as having a singular, permanent, or autonomous entity themselves? All things defy the synthetic attributes we use to define them, such as being existent or nonexistent, true or false, real or unfindable.

If you leave the ordinary definitions of emptiness aside, you may find that the concept is much friendlier than you previously thought—and easier to understand too. In fact, the descriptive term *open-dimensionality* is one translator's informative interpretation of emptiness, by the way. It's as if you could almost say that emptiness is full, because when you see the open-dimensional nature of things, you understand that emptiness includes the connectedness, poignancy, and warmth of being alive.

When we speak of wisdom in the Mahayana Buddhist tradition, it refers to insight into the nature of emptiness. Such wisdom describes your ability to enjoy and feel touched by the poignancy of life without trying to capture or reject it. No appearance can outshine the wisdom that knows emptiness. The mind that knows emptiness does not mistake the map for the territory or cling to rightness or truth. It clearly sees the interconnected relationship of things without losing the bigger picture by fixating on realness. Wisdom here describes the experience of finding your place in the infinite nature of contingency. A deep sanity arises from this. This experience of sanity is what I mean when I say grace.

Perhaps by now, you can see that even at the start of this book, as we began to question the limitations of rightness, we were already stepping into the wisdom of knowing emptiness. We have been talking about emptiness the whole time, in fact.

THE TWO TRUTHS: NOT TWO OR TRUE

It has never existed as anything whatsoever, yet arises as anything at all.

—Longchenpa, *The Basic Space of Phenomena*

By now, you may feel at least *somewhat* convinced that things don't possess intrinsic characteristics from their own side. You may have even had some direct experiences of looking and not finding, and glimpsed the illusory nature of appearance. Yet like most people you probably find it challenging to question, say, the many political or ethical principles that you have an emotional or intellectual investment in. Perhaps it feels like a denial to question the assumptions you have around some deeply personal truths, for example, those you have developed concerning the circumstances of your own personal history.

You may conclude: Emptiness is all very well and good, but what about climate change? Don't tell me that *that* doesn't exist. Don't tell me that my sister doesn't have cancer or that my wife is not having an affair, that my back doesn't hurt, or that I'm not in love. And, especially, don't tell me that Republicans have a better political agenda than Democrats. Any sane and well-adjusted person—like me—would have to agree that such things are true.

When we separate the spiritual from the temporal in this way, we prevent insight from infiltrating delusion. In other words, there is no way to work with the nature of interdependent expression if we reify it. This dividing of spiritual insight from the "realities" of everyday life makes spirituality seem impractical and only suitable for those who are out of touch. "Yes," you may argue, "meditation and prayer may help me relax and find balance, but aside from that, they have no place for those of us who live in the real world and deal with real problems."

It is important to understand that when we are questioning things—particularly the painful or challenging circumstances we face as individuals and societies—we are not dismissing life as it presents itself to us. What we are questioning, however, is the way in which we look at things. For instance, issues such as climate change are not singular, permanent, or independent things, as we have discussed at length; they are instead open-dimensional, dynamic, and subjectively known. Our great challenge as human beings is to learn how to reconcile the nature of things with their expression.

A brilliant and renowned eighteenth-century Tibetan Buddhist scholar, Je Mipham Rinpoche, addressed the artificial split between the spiritual and the temporal by comparing it to the behavior of an elephant. Elephants roll in the water to wash off the dirt and then roll in the dirt to dry off. His example humorously dramatizes the expression of a deep misunderstanding: that we have to choose between something being right or wrong, real or unreal; that we have no other option but to affirm or deny experience; and that there is no possibility of reconciling the temporal and the spiritual. This binary model, which we so often adhere to, is described in the Buddhist tradition as "the confusion of dualistic thinking." Looking at things through the lens of true and untrue, as we have been discussing throughout this book, is not the most nuanced approach to life.

Mipham Rinpoche was deeply influenced by a great master who lived many centuries before him, Nagarjuna. You might call Nagarjuna a spiritual genius because his understanding of interdependence was deeply refined, but his insight didn't simply remain in the realm of his intellect. For him, pratityasamutpada came alive with the experience of liberation. That means that he could see the illusory and magical nature of interdependence, so he experienced unlimited freedom without a trace of misunderstanding. And the way in which he presented the teachings on pratityasamutpada rocked the Mahayana Buddhist world.

Nagarjuna entered the scene somewhere around the second century and is known as the patriarch of the Madhyamaka or Middle Way School. Nagarjuna recognized that the teachings on dependent arising lay at the very epicenter of Buddha's path and developed and clarified their meaning, reenergizing the teachings of the Mahayana tradition.

Nagarjuna relied upon a model or framework that helped reconcile a deep misunderstanding we have about the nature of reality, called the Two Truths. The Two Truths are distinctly known as the relative and absolute truth.

Relative truth is a convenient label for anything that expresses itself, that moves or occurs, that can be known or is knowing itself, and so on, due to its relationship with other things. Of course, as we have been exploring, that is pretty much everything you can perceive or imagine, because nothing lies outside the nature of pratityasamutpada. You could define relative truth as that which only finds meaning, defining characteristics, value, and efficacy in reliance upon an other. So relative things possess no intrinsic truth at all but rather have a provisional function in particular contexts. In short, if you understand that everything leans, you naturally understand the meaning of the relative truth.

The absolute truth, on the other hand, is a conventional term for the unfindable nature or open-dimensionality of things. Although the nature of all relative appearance is empty (in that nothing possesses intrinsic characteristics from its own side), there is really no reason to deny experience on a relative, practical level. Emptiness does not negate appearance. Things are simply empty *because* they are mutually dependent. To assume that things intrinsically possess objective characteristics is to misunderstand their very nature. To misperceive the nature of appearance is the basis for deception, delusion, and reactivity. If, on the other hand, you remember the open-dimensionality of experience, the absolute truth of emptiness, it will inform your actions, and you will be able to respond to life based on seeing clearly.

There is no essential conflict between the relative and the absolute truth, in the same way that there is no conflict between the appearance of a rainbow and its unfindable nature. Emptiness and appearance seem to oppose each other only when we artificially separate the nature of things from their appearance. They come into conflict only when we think things have to be either real or unreal, when we think that our only option is to affirm or deny them or decide whether something is or is not. My suggestion is this: remove the conjunction *or* from these equations and frame it differently.

An effective way to speak of the relationship between relative and absolute truth would be to use the word *because* (instead of *or*) and state it in this way: "It is *because* everything leans that all things are empty of defining characteristics." In other words, it is because we can't find anything that exists outside the nature of contingent relationship that all things are free or empty of the restricting labels we assign to them.

We can also flip this equation around and look at it from the other unopposing side. We can say, "It is *because* everything is empty or free of defining truths that the world of infinite expression *can* arise, unhindered." Something that was not empty and that possessed its own intrinsic characteristics would by definition lie outside the nature of contingent relationships. Such a thing would be a closed system and couldn't be in relationship with anything, in which case you would never encounter it. Nothing would move—everything would be inert. You couldn't experience anything because (not being in relationship with anything else) it would not be knowable. Who could speak of such a thing?

So I want to emphasize *because* as the operative word here, in that it aids us in conceptually framing the relationship between nature and appearance. It helps us understand that the relative truth has always been simpatico with emptiness. This was emphatically stated in the single most renowned Buddhist text—the *Heart Sutra*—when the Buddha, via Avalokiteshvara, revealed to his disciple Shariputra, "Form is emptiness, emptiness is form. Form is no other than emptiness, emptiness is no other than form."

What this means is that there is no conflict between the appearance of a thing and its unfindability. In fact, upon looking at things in this way, you cannot say appearance and emptiness are one, but you cannot say they are two either—you cannot say they are the same, and you can't say they are separate. They share a relationship similar to water and ice. You can't separate ice from water, yet you cannot say they are the same either. When you look into the nature of appearance, you will find that all things are empty of an independent reality. And due to this very absence of true existence, the world of appearances expresses itself through the nature of dependent arising. The entire purpose of the Middle Way investigative tradition is to understand this extraordinary equation.

Ironically, what Nagarjuna called the Two Truths are not actually two; nor are they true but rather a way of framing experience that allows us to reconcile its two seemingly distinct aspects: the way things appear and function, and their actual mode of being, or nature. He refers to them as the Two Truths to give our dualistic mind something to work with. Yet as you may see, they are not separate but simply a way of speaking about aspects of the fullness of experience.

In fact, Nagarjuna even made a special point in warning us of the dangers of clinging to either of the truths as true. The relative truth can't be found upon investigation. And the so-called absolute truth is simply not a thing. The absolute truth points to the experience of knowing the nature and appearance of things in an unconfused way. So to cling to the absolute as true would turn the antidote—insight into the empty nature of reality—into a thing or dogma, in which case there could be no seeing through delusion. The mind would have to close down in order to know or reify its object in such a way that it would impede clear seeing. What would be the use of this kind of realization?

It would be most useful to see Nagarjuna's teachings on the Two Truths as a means or tool—rather than a truth—that helps us use prajna, or accurate discernment, to penetrate misunderstandings we have about the way things are. It is practical, by design. It challenges the mind that thinks like an elephant, which is what is needed for insight to occur. The wisdom that comes from seeing the empty nature of things will continue to disrupt the mind that clings to truths—and that's its beauty.

3

Faith

BEYOND BELIEF AND DOUBT

FAITHING

Take care that you don't reach conclusions, so that you can understand the incomprehensible.

—Saint Bonaventure

We have been exploring how, because everything leans, the world doesn't lend itself to being known in a determinate way. Humbling, isn't it? To live with humility and curiosity has a lot to do with faith. Faith implies that there is something we don't know—if we already knew, we wouldn't need faith in the first place. But there is more to faith than simply not knowing. The term *faith* conveys a sense of confidence in the face of not knowing, a deep appreciation for mystery and wonder, and a longing to be touched by life rather than withdrawing from or thinking you can fix it.

As I said earlier, I would like to introduce a working definition of faith that gets to the heart of the human condition. Faith, as I present it here, is not something you have or you don't, or something you need to acquire. Rather, it is a way of engaging life: it's active, more like a verb, as in, *faith-ing*. In other words, let's entertain faith not as a truth but as a practice or a way of being.

We have spent a lot of time investigating the nature of things. We have done a lot of looking and not finding, which has led to the insight that life—by virtue of its open-dimensional nature—defies definition. To recognize and live in accord with this realization is to faith. Faith has a quality of giving over to something greater than the limited world of your beliefs and doubts. But it doesn't demand that you blindly give over agency to something outside of yourself, far from it. Faithing is a playful exchange that transpires between your own discernment and the world you experience. It is intuitive and responsive. You might, at any time, encounter something that touches you and evokes a sense of humility and curiosity in your mind. But the object encountered alone is not what causes faith to arise. *You* have to recognize the object as something of value. Recognition, inspiration, and appreciation arise as natural qualities of your own mind. You can understand faithing as a dance between your so-called inner and outer worlds.

Faithing expresses the pursuit of grace in relationship. This path begins the moment you begin to wonder about your place in the great nature of infinite contingency. This was the Buddha's intention. In the sutras he cautioned us not to hold on to the path as a truth, but rather a means. He asked, "Does a boatman carry the boat on his back having reached the opposite shore?" He wanted us to consider that, like a boat, our path serves as a vehicle that transports us beyond confused reactive mind. He encouraged us to see the path as a moving and lively endeavor, not a truth or dogma to cling to. The path and our allegiance to it then become a living dynamic experience.

Whether you engage in a formal spiritual practice or not, you must tread your own path, and that requires that you relate to the world in which you live. No matter how much you resist the whole idea of faith, you will never find a way to remove yourself from the nature of pratityasamutpada, which means you will never know anything in a definitive way. In understanding this, faith makes perfect sense. Sure, you can try to hang on to being right. Of course, you don't have to let go into humbleness. You probably hang on a lot. But in the end, you will need to ask yourself if hanging on provides you with the security you seek. In fact, grasping for security in a world in which everything leans is a setup for doubt, disappointment, and stress.

Faithing, on the other hand, offers us a place of rest and confidence. But it is a different kind of confidence—one founded on humility and openness. By humility I am not referring to feeling small or diminished, in the way that we often describe as being like a "doormat." Humility here refers to freedom from rightness and reification. This kind of open humility protects you from being stuck. So even though the process of living may prove itself rugged and challenging at times—undoubtedly you will have your share of bumping up against unwanted circumstances—you can be sure, if you stay open, that the world will teach you as you go, and you will feel alive.

We have explored faith as an individual experience, but we can also approach the topic as a cultural narrative. Nowadays, in many circles, *faith* has become a bad word. People reject whole lineages of wisdom because they associate faith with extremism or backward thinking. You can find a broad spectrum of cultural disillusionment around faith when it comes to things like organized religion or the institution of marriage. You may put a lot of stock in these things too, until you come face-to-face with the messiness of your own and others' humanness.

Of course, such disappointments arise from failed expectations, so in a sense you were doomed from the start. Because you believed, you had nowhere to go but to fall into doubt. You didn't really understand that life never agreed to cooperate with your sense of justice. What you might call "the church," "my spouse," or "my body" was never some singular, permanent, or independent entity you could take refuge in. The cynicism and disappointment that you may have felt around faith came from misunderstanding the nature of things from the very beginning.

Nowadays many people associate faith with fundamentalism and dogma, but if you look at the quality of these experiences, you find an awful lot of expectations and rightness. Holding on to rightness and letting go into humbleness, or faithing, reflect two very different ways in which we respond to the human condition. Fundamentalism comes from attempting to find a lasting refuge in a moving world. It doesn't possess the flexibility that embraces a diversity of ideas and experiences. You can explore for yourself the difference between feeling right and the confidence that comes from your ability to accept the full and unknowable nature of life. To accept things as they are—to faith—brings a deep sense of ease, insight, bravery, and compassion. You might even begin to wonder if you have any choice but to faith.

Looking at words and experiences as closely as we have been doing unpacks the assumptions that might otherwise remain locked up in language. Thoughts and ideas are powerful, and they dictate how we see the world and the direction we move in. To make clear distinctions between rightness, fundamentalism, or expectation and genuine faith releases us from vague assumptions and provides us with the choice to clearly investigate and work with the human predicament. Our ability to faith—or not—plays a fundamental role in determining the quality of our well-being.

So let's not just write faith off so glibly. After all, it's not faith's fault that we use it as a synonym for expectation, dogma, or rightness. Even the greatest cynics and conspiracy theorists—those who resist the very notion of faith—have faith in their ideas. As long as you are breathing and your heart is pumping in your chest, you will never escape the need to faith, and why would you want to? The human predicament literally pushes at you day after day, calling to your courage and intelligence, imploring you to pay attention to life as it is, urging you to let go into humbleness. How long can you ignore it?

BELIEF

In the early modern period, Western people fell in love with an ideal of absolute certainty that, it seems, may be unattainable.

But because some are reluctant to relinquish it, they have tended to overcompensate, claiming certitude for beliefs and doctrines that can only be provisional.

—Karen Armstrong, *The Case for God*

Once, while my friend Maryanne and I were out riding our horses together in the open plains of the San Luis Valley in southern Colorado, she asked me if I believed in reincarnation. I struggled with that question, not because of the reincarnation part but because of the way in which she used the term *belief*. It's kind of a setup. To ask, "Do you believe?" forces the answerer into making a choice between true or false—into affirming or denying something—which ultimately comes down to being right or wrong about how things actually are. For me, this use of the term *belief* presents a limited way of looking at things, a departure from the more open, inquisitive qualities of mind that I have come to appreciate through my years of investigative practice.

People often say things like, "I believe in God." Or they might believe in the Buddha, in heaven, or karma. Some people only believe what they see with their own two eyes. Sometimes—especially in songs—people say, "I believe in love." But just believing in love doesn't compare to the experience of extending or experiencing love. It does not address the condition of heartbreak, loss of a loved one, the complexity of relationships, or the irony that although most people value love, we simply do not find enough of it in our world. As we have explored through analytical investigation, while you can hold on to beliefs as truths, they will never correspond to the full and dynamic nature of things. Beliefs are not hands-on or exploratory enough to allow for that.

I don't want to define belief for you. There is no right or wrong here. Language in itself never makes anything true; it only provides a channel for communication and exploration. I bring this all up because I just want to encourage you to think about how you use the term. Like me, you may find the word *belief* to be an inadequate way of communicating what you value or experience. In other contexts, belief may work perfectly well for you. The term *belief*, for my friend Maryanne, may have had a completely different meaning than it does for me. For instance, belief can be an idea with a strong sense of direction. You may say, "I believe in you," when encouraging a friend to forge ahead with her vision to go back to school, climb a mountain, or pull herself out of a depression. "You can do it!"

Belief doesn't have to concretize. In India, for instance, it's common to walk past a tree with an interesting knot in a branch and find that someone has already been there and left a flower offering. Someone felt moved, and that person responded. In such cases, belief expressed itself as a sense of wonder, respect, and appreciation for the movement and mystery of life.

It is worth looking into the etymology of the word *belief*, which people often use interchangeably with the term *faith*. In her book *The Case for God*, Karen Armstrong explains that when the New Testament was translated into Latin in the fourth century, the word used for the Greek *pisteo* ("I believe") was the Latin word *credo*, which then carried a meaning something like, "I give my heart." The King James Bible used the English word *believe* from the German *belieben*, which meant "to value," "to hold dear," or "to pledge allegiance through service." In religious contexts, *to believe* referred to the belief in a specific doctrine.

In the late seventeenth century, a time historians call the early modern period, an entirely new kind of civilization emerged, governed by scientific rationality and based on capital investment. We began to use the term *belief* to describe the mental acceptance of facts, rather than to talk about a response to the movement and mystery of the world around us. What we couldn't pin down we began to dismiss as superstitious or naive. From this point of view, we relegated faith to mythology, whereas facts and empiricism belonged to the pragmatic and realistic thinker concerned with truth.

Looking through the lens of whether something is true or not reduces the fullness and mystery of life to an idea, a subjective conclusion. After all, is not the assumption that what you think or perceive is true also a giant leap of faith?

My sister-in-law, Dickey Lama, once told me a story. She was born in India, the daughter of Tibetan parents, and grew up listening to the hagiographies of the great Buddhist saints as bedtime stories. But like so many others of her generation, Dickey also received a Western education and so possesses the critical intelligence that necessarily comes with living in contemporary culture.

One day she brought home for her mother a local, low-budget video that a neighbor had made, which depicted the life of Padmasambhava, the Tibetan saint who brought Buddhism to Tibet from India in the seventh century. Spiritual biographies describe him as magical. He could fly and appear in many places at once. He would hide sacred scriptures among the natural elements, such as rocks and the ethers of space, to ensure the preservation of the Buddhist teachings for future generations. He displayed unconventional behavior, drank alcohol, wrathfully subdued negative forces, and was known for having many spiritual consorts.

In one of his many famous adventures, Padmasambhava wandered into a kingdom in northern India and took up with the king's daughter, who happened to be a nun. The king expressed his displeasure by commanding his minions to prepare a pile of wood upon which to burn Padmasambhava. But the hero wouldn't burn. Instead, the surrounding area transformed into a lake, and Padmasambhava remained unscathed. Humbled, the king offered him his crown and robes.

You may wonder how a local group of amateur neighborhood filmmaker-producers pulled this scene off. The actor-protagonist in the drama stood in the center of a pile of wood, in which had been woven pieces of red, yellow, and orange crepe paper to give the illusion of fire. They placed a fan nearby to blow air onto the set, which made the paper wave and crackle. You could hear it whirring throughout the scene in the background. Naturally, having seen many well-produced Hollywood films, my sister-in-law couldn't get past the bad filmmaking and started to laugh. But when she turned around, she saw her mother deeply moved, tears streaming down her face.

This story vividly illustrates the differences in worldviews that can bring about vastly different interpretations of the same experience. Dickey told me this story with the utmost respect for this direct and humble way of responding to life, so prevalent in the older generation of Tibetans and other indigenous cultures. From a contemporary point of view it may seem naive, but if you witness these qualities of openness and aliveness, it makes you realize you have something to learn from "the old way." As people of contemporary culture we arrogantly assume that we have a better grasp on reality. But wouldn't a more believable Hollywood production have just offered a more polished illusion?

Beliefs bind you when they cut off the flow of your curiosity. You can count on beliefs, such as "People of faith are naive," "Bob is the perfect boyfriend," or "The world is a mess," to bring an abrupt halt to the liveliness of an inquiry. Beliefs are vague approximations—like maps—that, if mistaken as true, block you from the primacy of experience. Yes, you can find a lot of evidence that the world is a mess, but if you make that a belief, you will miss out on a lot of extraordinary happenings in the process: all those luminous sunrises, all those moments when people bravely put aside their self-concern to serve others in need, all the exotic bird-mating dances, funny jokes, and uncontrollable laughter. You will miss an autumn leaf drop from a tree, a meteor shower, or a moment of awe. And yes, there is heartbreak too. Who could argue with that? But you can't accurately say that heartbreak is all there is.

It may be that life's abundance overwhelms you. We are not habituated to the unbearable fullness of being. When you feel encumbered by uncertainty, when you feel threatened or hurt, you may prefer to secure yourself in the rightness of your story, default to blame, or conclude that the world is a miserable place. This is an effective way of withdrawing from life. Yes, you can hold on to your views—that's one way to go—but just know you have the option to go in a more empowered direction. You have the choice to step outside the boundaries of true and untrue and to experience life's limitless glory.

Let's return to Maryanne's question about reincarnation. At the heart of her query lies the assumption that the self presently exists and that at some point in time you will fall into extinction. But how did this self come into being in the first place? Did it just suddenly, spontaneously appear from mere nothingness without causes and conditions? If so, when did its nonthingness end and its thingness begin? You may trace the thingness back to many causes and conditions, but when you do this, you may not find a singular, permanent, or independent entity at all. In fact, you will keep bumping into the nature of infinite contingency. So at what point will this self—this thing you can't find—become a nothing? And at death, where would a nothing go?

As intellectual as this may sound, our relationship with existence and extinction is a deep-rooted emotional belief. And it's a belief that begets fear. Everyone is haunted by loss, separation, and death. You have an intimate relationship to this sense of autonomous, singular, and permanent existence functioning in a mode of constant survival—a desperate attempt to hold on to ground and the fear of losing it. The stronger you hold on, the more you feel burdened by stress, anxiety, and the fear of extinction and loss.

But if you begin to look at reincarnation as an inquiry, it will transport you out of the restricted paradigm of is and is not. And it will create room for something lively and intelligent to occur. When I look at reincarnation in this way, I see that it serves a powerful function in directing the way I understand and live my life. It helps me see beyond my idea of myself as a singular and separate I that will, at some unknown point, fall into extinction. And seeing beyond this brings me closer to the beauty, fullness, and mystery of life, something unrestricted by the notions of me, the extinction of me—or even the reincarnation of me. For this reason, I see no need to believe or disbelieve in reincarnation.

DOUBT

If I ever become a Saint—I will surely be one of "darkness." I will continually be absent from Heaven—to light the light of those in darkness on earth.

—Mother Teresa of Calcutta

In my late thirties I entered into a long retreat at our community retreat land in Crestone, Colorado. I remember at one point, as I sat on the edge of the bed in my retreat cabin, high up on the side of a mountain, I looked out the window and felt a painful distance from my meditation practice. I longed for a feeling of inspiration, devotion, or compassion, but none arose. What do you do when you encounter a spiritual dry spell or confront rough, unwanted experiences? What happens when spirituality shows up in a way that doesn't feel comfortable for you, when doubts arise, when someone in the spiritual community does something that you don't understand, or when you just can't access the warmth of your practice?

As my retreat progressed, I began to look into these questions. My struggle, I observed, was instigated by subtle preferences I had about what I should or shouldn't feel. These shoulds and shouldn'ts sprung from a belief that faith was something I ought to always feel, under any circumstances, in order to be a good Buddhist. But it came to me clearly at this time that this type of good did not include the full spectrum of my humanness. What was I to do with that?

I came across Mother Teresa's published letters, and I remember feeling oddly inspired by her description of long periods of desolation and estrangement from God. I thought, "Who could have more faith and dedication to her spiritual path than Mother Teresa?" The publication of her intimate journals revealed a crisis of faith, dark nights of the soul. When I thought of Mother Teresa's plight, I wondered if it might not have been her opportunity to go beyond the limiting notions she had about the God she so longed for, to a full and unconditional faith. Rather than seeing her as a one-dimensional icon of virtue, suddenly she came alive for me as someone who was confronting her own dualistic notions of shoulds and shouldn'ts: what God should look like, how she should experience him, what the culmination of her many years of courageous service should look like.

Of course, this is all conjecture on my part. I have no personal knowledge of Mother Teresa's inner journey or of how it all finally played out. But I like to imagine that her doubt did indeed push her beyond the limiting notions she had about the divine to an unconditional sort of faith, which embraced the full expression of her human condition. Inspired by Mother Teresa's profound conundrum, I started to reflect on the opportunity doubt provided me as well.

Doubt, like any other word, can be understood in any number of ways. Doubt can be a question—a way into exploring something you might otherwise take for granted. For instance, in the context of this book, you could say that we are questioning that things may not exist as they appear, which opens up an entire investigation into the nature of appearance. We have seen that in doubting the truth of your own story, you protect yourself from the reactivity and confusion that emerges from assuming you are right.

Doubt often presents itself with an initial discomfort; something feels off, unwholesome, or threatening. Doubt will challenge your sacred cows, everything you hold dear. It poses a risk: the entire edifice of a belief is in danger of collapsing at any moment, which can be scary—petrifying even. That's because doubt and belief share the same bed: when our beliefs don't hold up, there is doubt; and when we fear meaninglessness, there is belief. There is something fragile about the whole system.

It takes a lot of faith to explore doubt. But you might detect, like I did, a sacredness and opportunity that resides within its darkness. Doubt will lay things bare. It will strip you of your self-deception. And, of course, that is when and how authentic spiritual growth takes place—or at least it can. That will depend on what you do next.

There is a fine line that separates doubt as a belief and doubt as an open question. Doubt as a belief has already concretized its object. As we have discussed, the process goes as follows: you detect something is off, and your story begins to congeal; you have already decided what something is or is not, and the emotional stirrings of rightness begin to reveal themselves. All of a sudden the door to faithing closes, along with any sense of awe or possibility.

On the other hand, if you are up for it, you can do something different. You can use doubt as an opportunity, by allowing yourself access to your own curiosity. The mind poised for insight is not afraid to question because it does not cling to truth, judge, or reify its object. Rather, it possesses the qualities of agility, attentiveness, and skepticism. You may associate skepticism with doubt and cynicism, but surprisingly the term *skepticism* has its origin in the Greek word, *skeptikoi*, which means "to suspend judgment." The proponents of classical philosophical skepticism practiced open-mindedness, suspending both belief and doubt. They understood that by not clinging to truths, you have nothing to lose. So go ahead: question away!

I want to give doubt a wide girth here because it is something for you to explore. For me, doubt has been a poignant and challenging part of my path, and I have come to see that it has the potential to go in many directions. But I do want to continue asking you to pay attention to the difference between doubts as concretized assumptions and doubts as a means to instigate an inquiry. As you begin to distinguish more clearly the difference, you may even enjoy observing your mind open, then close, and then open again. It is a joy to see both. This kind of investigation strengthens your ability to faith.

In these times, it seems to me that the topic of doubt needs more exploration. Traditionally (and still in many contexts) it was not a good thing to even question beliefs, let alone doubt them. Nowadays, however, it seems many people take pride in doubt and even try to cultivate it. In contemporary culture we tend to associate cynicism with intelligence; you find a lot of intellectual arrogance associated with doubt. Those who run on this kind of intellectual doubt often think faith is beneath them, that to have faith is simpleminded and blind.

Perhaps, but beware: doubt can be riddled with assumptions. What doubt often provides is essentially just another set of beliefs. Asserting that something is not true is just as much a belief as thinking that it is true. Doubters can be just as zealous as believers.

When your beliefs are threatened, you probably want to take cover, hole up in a fortress, put on a bulletproof vest, fight back. And when you are physically threatened, such tactics may indeed be a wise strategy. But clinging to doubt is a rejection of life. There is no true comfort in it. Ironically, unconditional protection can only come from faithing.

I don't want to underestimate the confusion and despair that often accompanies doubt. Doubt can isolate you from individuals and communities. It can leave you feeling alone in the dark, frozen or completely immobilized. And, like belief, it doesn't necessarily need a logical basis. Most often it finds sustenance from unexamined assumptions, emotional turbulence, and insecurity. If you look into doubt, you will find many things: that it keeps you from accessing the positivity or the brightness of your mind, that it can make you feel jagged or physically depressed and out of balance. It may cause you to feel disconnected from your spiritual path or your loved ones. Doubt might even make you feel doomed to suffer—but that's impossible.

Even amid all of your confusion you still have one thing going for you. You are tethered to the path of awakening simply because you long for happiness and freedom from suffering. Even in times of extreme isolation, when you feel engulfed by darkness and uncertainty, when you feel estranged from a sense of well-being, you will never escape your natural inclination and longing for unconditional freedom. The contemporary Buddhist teacher Anam Thubten puts it this way: "You are doomed for enlightenment."

In the moments you're able to free yourself from the dualism of belief and doubt, you may come to value the way life presents itself to you as something to learn from. Who is to say how God or one's spiritual path should look? Could it be that Mother Teresa's darkest encounters were the face of God and not his absence? As I moved deeper into my retreat I began to see how clinging to notions of how my practice should look was no different from my modus operandi of just trying to survive in the world by getting what I wanted, living around unwanted experiences, and trying to maintain some semblance of security in their midst. There is a courage that comes from this insight because one no longer finds oneself at the mercy of one's preferences. The beauty and kindness of faithing is that it does not demand that you experience anything other than what you experience. It turns out that I didn't have to transcend my humanness to find genuine confidence. Rather, I came to see that my purpose as a spiritual practitioner was to increase my ability to be fully human.

ETERNALISM: GETTING TO THE BOTTOM OF THINGS

The view of dependent origination exposes all Eternalistic and Nihilistic views.

—Nagarjuna

Throughout history people have been searching for the meaning of existence, making assertions about the origin of the universe, and attempting to come to terms with the inevitability of their own extinction. As a youngster, not long after you learned to speak in sentences, you probably started asking your parents some important questions concerning existence and causation, such as, "Where does outer space begin?" "Why is the sky blue?" or "Who or what created the universe?"

As an adult you may look toward science, religion, or philosophy for answers to these same questions. Our quest for meaning and our longing to make sense of both existence and death extend beyond the boundaries of time and culture. For instance, if you were to research the many philosophical systems in practice at the time of the Buddha, you would find that they resemble the same ones you encounter in the world today. Human culture trends toward ontological beliefs, such as a divine presence of one or multiple Gods, an unbreakable particle, or a primal energetic substance that serves as the building block for grosser matter, a Spirit or Universal Self, or a Consciousness that permeates all experience.

If we were to consider all these as a whole, they represent a search for a singular source, an ultimate cause, truth, or explanation that would answer the many questions we have about consciousness, matter, and the human condition. "Perhaps we will find that one miracle, that one singular cause," we think, "and everything will make sense."

Individually and culturally we have come up with some spectacular explanations for why the world is how it is. For instance, science offers a clear explanation for why the sky appears blue. The blueness of the sky is determined by the way the atmosphere interacts with sunlight, which is made up of a full spectrum of colors. Light waves refract, bend, and change speed as they pass through various media. We see color based upon the mechanics of how the human eye functions and takes in information, and we filter and organize all this sensory data by way of our nervous system.

But try as you may, you will never get to the bottom of why the sky is blue, why the human eye is designed the way it is, why the sun emits so many colors, why things are configured and function as they do. You may pin these on a singular source or system of creation, but that will only lead to more questions, such as: "Well, who created that cause? What is that made of?" If you look in a linear way for an answer to these questions, you will get caught in a mode of infinite regress. You will never get to the bottom of things or reach a final conclusion.

Furthermore, your questions themselves—the notions of blue, why, and sky—come from language agreements that only have meaning in the context of human sensibilities. These words and ideas are not truths unto themselves but frameworks through which you can evaluate and explore things. They are part of your investigation, and when coupled with deep interest, they can open up your world like fractals into the great nature of contingency. You will emerge, as if from a narrow tunnel, into a perspective unhindered by the limiting concept of a linear, singular source of causation.

Perhaps, having spent a bit of time looking and not finding, you do feel a growing sense of confidence that nothing exists outside the nature of interdependence. But just for argument's sake, let's imagine that you could find an eternal thing as the original source or cause of all existence and everything we think and feel. What characteristics would it have? For starters, as we know, it would have to exist as singular, unchanging, and completely independent. More to the point, in order for such a thing to maintain its eternal status, it could have no discernible beginning or end because it would have no connection to causes and conditions. In addition, such a thing would necessarily have to exist as complete or whole, which means it could not be comprised of parts. It would naturally follow that such a thing would resist analysis and would remain immune to or unaffected by the movement and energy of mutual causality.

But how would such a thing then create a universe? It would have no agency or efficacy. In order to create a universe, this eternal thing would have to depart from its independent status to join the nature of infinite relationship. So, you see, this hypothetical thing that could not be perceived or known by virtue of its independent nature would lie entirely outside the realm of experience. How could you know it?

You might recall that earlier in the book we took on Carl Sagan's challenge to make an apple pie from scratch, and we couldn't find a singular source for its creation. We couldn't identify where the apple pie left off and the world began. Through the same kind of investigation, you will come to realize that not only can you not make an apple pie from scratch, but you cannot make a universe from scratch either.

I want to explain why the investigation of faith is important to me in relation to eternalism. I admit I have a personal agenda here. I am concerned with the purity and authenticity of the Buddha's wisdom, which is not immune to our human tendency toward rightness and dogma. I want to play my small part in protecting the brilliance of this tradition from the insidious tendency we all have to shut down around definitive conclusions. Furthermore, I want to honor the original spirit and intent of all the world's wisdom lineages, which—before they were concretized into systems of belief—emerged from human experiences of awe and grace.

For this reason, it is important to explore eternalism. Eternalism—which might also be called realism or essentialism—does not refer to a specific ideology, philosophical tradition, or religion, but rather originates in the human longing to seek truth, security, and answers to the tough and mysterious questions we have about reality. Our search for knowledge and inner peace reflects the nobility and beauty of human curiosity. The problem, known as eternalism as we refer to it in the Buddhist teachings, begins with the quest for something real or essential. This creates problems because such a search is not in accord with the nature of dependent arising. We cannot find ultimate truths in the world of relationship. Clinging to ideological truths undermines our ability to faith.

In the tradition of pratityasamutpada, the texts describe the genesis of our confusion as coming from our inability to bear the fullness of the nature of infinite contingency. This misunderstanding gives "true" a platform. True serves as the terra firma for belief. Belief supports rightness, and from there generates a cycle of fundamentalism, fear, and confusion.

You may think of fundamentalism as religious extremism, but it isn't necessarily tied to religion. Fundamentalism results from assuming things intrinsically exist as they appear to you, and this impedes any possibilities for genuine learning and clear communication. As we know all too well, extreme rightness expresses itself on a global scale. As fundamentalism continues to increase and intensify around the world, faithing becomes more important than ever before. We can unite around what we have in common as a species, which is that ultimately we don't know: we can't find a singular source of creation or any determinate truth to stand on. Faith offers a practice of humility that serves as a critical refuge from the confusion of fundamentalism and doubt and the myriad ways they influence human actions and often cause harm.

I have some close friends who, in a tongue-in-cheek kind of way, proclaim to be "Buddhist fundamentalists." They say this out of a fierce allegiance to the unique wisdom of this practice tradition. If being a Buddhist fundamentalist means deeply valuing the fundamentals of Buddhist wisdom and appreciating the nature of pratityasamutpada, then I would also have to call myself a Buddhist fundamentalist. But we usually don't use the term in that way. In truth, there is really no such thing as a Buddhist fundamentalist—that is, if you practice the Buddhist teachings in an authentic way. Even holding on to the most altruistic aspects of the Buddha's path as right interferes with the vitality and spirit of open inquiry. Open inquiry is not exclusively Buddhist, although the Buddha taught it explicitly as the spirit and approach of the path. What we are talking about here is not a religious issue but a deeply human one.

If you look at the early sutras of the Buddhist tradition, you will find teaching examples on the dangers of concretizing wisdom into beliefs. This shows us that even at the time of the Buddha some very earnest practitioners misunderstood the essential meaning of pratityasamutpada.

My teacher has often told the story of two virtuous monks who attended a discourse by the Buddha and received an introduction to emptiness for the first time. Prior to this, both virtuously observed and studied the laws of karma, cause and effect, interdependence, and impermanence, and religiously honored their vows and precepts. But instead of seeing these practices as a means of liberation, they clung to them as definitive truths. As the Buddha spoke of the empty nature of all things, including karma and interdependence, the monks misconstrued the meaning of his words to mean that emptiness was a complete annihilation of everything they believed in. Consequently, as the story goes, they went into shock, had heart attacks, and died.

Such parables emerged as Buddhism developed and blossomed in India, and as the teachings on emptiness became more explicit and prominent. Some of these teachings, such as the one about the two monks, poke fun at a less refined or partial understanding of the Buddha's teachings on interdependence. But their purpose is to clarify the original intent of the Buddha, which was his teaching on the genuine and complete meaning of pratityasamutpada: "a matter hard to perceive, namely this conditionality, this pratityasamutpada . . . against the stream of common thought, deep, subtle, difficult, delicate."[1]

The wisdom of interdependence provides supreme protection from fundamentalism. As we saw, for the two monks in the story, this conundrum was not merely a philosophical issue but a deeply emotional one because they saw it as a destruction of their beliefs. Grasping and fixating on ideas in this way challenges our ability to genuinely faith. Fear of annihilation comes as the counterpart to eternalism, which we will address in the next section.

What is so beautiful about pratityasamutpada is that while you can't locate a singular eternal thing—and therefore it follows that no idea, belief, or ideology could possibly be eternally true—such an insight does not deny the existence of the God you pray to; nor does it dismiss scientific discovery, the blueness of the sky, or the sacredness or power of any particular tradition. The world of relationship is powerful and effective despite its illusory nature. To live freely in the nature of interdependent expression, you don't have to give up the world you experience. All you have to give up is clinging to truth.

NIHILISM: IS THAT ALL THERE IS?

Investing non-things with qualities is like expounding on the beauty of a barren woman's daughter.

—Chandrakirti

Let me ask you: Have you ever experienced nothing? I think about this sometimes when I look up at the night sky and try to imagine the edge of the universe. It's hard to envision the other side of something. What exactly is nothing?

For me, nothing evokes images of endings: a dense cement wall beyond which is nothing, something that prevents me from moving ahead, a blackout or an abrupt halt of conscious experience. At other times, I envision nothing as an ever-expanding abyss. As I follow it, my conscious mind leaves behind everything it knows, stretching into referenceless space, severed from the warmth of relationship, lost.

Each time I try to imagine nothing, I encounter images, words, and moody atmospheres, which indicates to me that nothing is not a nonthing at all. Honestly, I don't recall ever having directly experienced a nonthing or a nonplace. And I suspect I (or you) never will. By definition, a nonthing can't have qualities, so how could you possibly know one? Yet the irony of all this is that most of us fear extinction or nothingness more than anything else.

I remember the exact moment as a young girl when I encountered the idea of nothingness: the idea that people and things disappeared and never came back. A neighborhood friend taught me about death—a word, she said, her mother told her never to say out loud in front of her younger brother. I recall sitting on the front porch of my house and the foreboding sense of doom that overcame me when I thought about the end of everything. Before this incident I knew the concept of "want but can't have" very well, but I had not yet been introduced to the concept of is and is not. It had never occurred to me to entertain such weighty ideas. As a child, you possess a natural longing to explain and make sense of the world—to find explanations for all the things that disturb or amaze you. Throughout your life you attribute meanings to these wondrous and puzzling encounters, influenced by preexisting language and attitudes you naturally absorb from your environment.

We can see that, even as children, we have stirrings of eternalistic and nihilistic leanings. Buddha referred to these tendencies as the *two extremes*. From a philosophical standpoint all formal religious or belief traditions fall to one side or the other. However, it is probably safe to say that no one can ever be a pure eternalist or a pure nihilist because one extreme will always cast the shadow of the other:

is always comes with isn't. We have already examined one half of the equation, eternalism, and couldn't find a singular, permanent, or independent thing. When you think about this more, it may make you wonder, "If I can't find an intrinsic thing, how is a nothing possible?" Hmmm . . . something more to investigate.

Nihilism first came into the philosophical vocabulary as a way of referring to particular weaknesses that accompanied specific systems of reasoning. No one actually wanted to become a nihilist. In fact, we might say that eternalism and nihilism both describe tendencies we fall into more than they express formal philosophical tenets. But they differ in their methods, focus, and conclusions.

If we can sum up eternalism as holding on to things and ideas as true, nihilism shows up when such beliefs fall apart and nothing makes sense. While eternalism is a term that describes the surety of existence, nihilism haunts us with the assurance of extinction and the severance from everything we hold dear. Nihilism moves us from the truth of a thing to a void, from rightness to doubt, from meaning to insignificance.

You might recognize nihilism in a worldview that argues against the value of ethical conduct or that doesn't see the need to connect the dots between cause and effect, to the point that conventional sensibilities get a bit wobbly. For example, we find strong traces of nihilism when we are told about the denial of anything beyond the material realm of our senses, which leads to a dismissal of metaphysics as a viable tool for understanding the nature of being. This sentiment represents the standard view of scientific materialism, which reduces the mysterious world of conscious experience to mere matter. This mechanistic view of reality implies that we have no freedom of choice and are bound to our biological impulses.

To summarize, eternalism strives to find substantial truths or to identify singular causes to explain why things are the way they are, whereas nihilism challenges objective truths through analysis or reductionism, which often leads to the rejection of the relative power of meaning and experience. Eternalism concretizes and nihilism destroys; eternalism affirms existence while nihilism affirms extinction; eternalism leans toward belief, while nihilism looks at the phenomenal world through doubt and negation.

As an attitude or mood, nihilism throws into suspicion our whole raison d'être. It most often leads to a dreary worldview that promises impending doom, as if you as an individual are all alone to forge your way through a bleak and unfriendly existence. Imagine a life devoid of meaning or purpose: "Why bother? It's a rigged game; we all have to die in the end anyway." That's nihilism. Of course, we all have moments of feeling ineffective or of falling into malaise, ennui, or numbness. But most people don't actively want to be nihilistic— it's not an uplifting way to walk through life.

Generally nihilism doesn't sound like much fun. But in some cases you may find in yourself a tendency to use the "nothing matters" logic to justify and indulge in all kinds of questionable activities. A nihilistic attitude will serve you well if all you want to do is party. It will provide the encouragement you need to do things that push against your conscience. "If nothing matters, why not just do whatever you want: let's drink and dance. Who cares?"

In 1969 Peggy Lee won a Grammy award for her nihilistic anthem: "Is That All There Is?" She sang: "If that's all there is, then let's keep dancing. Let's break out the booze and have a ball, if that's all there is." Cristina Monet-Palaci did a grittier, twisted version in 1980, which, because of its disturbing tone, became a punkish tribute to meaninglessness and existential angst. Of course, it was all tongue-in-cheek, but its gloomy atmospheric message summoned the menacing tendency we all have to lack purpose.

Curiously, views that eventually fall into nihilism often begin when someone dares to question the realness of something through analysis. You might start by questioning a belief, for instance, the belief that things have an intrinsic truth. After looking and not finding, your analysis might falter and then fall into nihilism rather than reveal a deeper insight. You may conclude then that life is devoid of meaning because things are unfindable. This is what happened in the story of the two monks we spoke of in the last section. In the context of Buddhist analytical meditation, a practitioner falls into nihilism when he or she mistakes emptiness as a state in which the power of cause and effect no longer function. It's as if, through the process of analysis, one has reduced the world of appearance and possibilities to dust. When the result of analysis ends in the annihilation of relative expression, one has officially fallen into nihilism.

It's actually humorous to think that just by probing the nature of things you would have the power to render something meaningless or nonexistent. Analysis doesn't have the power to destroy phenomena, to take away or give things inherent meaning. The values we place on objects derive their meaning in dependence on their contexts. It is relationship and relationship alone that defines the significance, characteristics, and function of experience. This is what we rely upon to navigate the world with grace. So analysis (or loosening practice, as we have been calling it) is nothing more than the playful process of learning from and marveling at the dynamic array of interdependent expression. Such an approach to analysis is not destined for nihilism.

What concerns me most about nihilism is that it leaves no room for wonder and humility. Nowadays many people place their faith in scientific materialism and have become disillusioned with the promise of organized religion. There are reasons for this kind of cynicism. People do all kinds of things in the name of faith that cause others to reject it. But be careful, because in one of its sneakiest and most harmful guises, nihilism expresses itself as the assumption that you can only trust what you perceive. One has only to stop and look around to know that there is more to life than what you experience in any given moment.

Nonetheless, the nihilist in all of us may at times fall into an apocalyptic view of the future; may contract around the fear of extinction and loss; may feel utterly alone and separate in the failure to recognize the richness and magic of the infinite world of interdependence; and may simply feel hopeless. Nihilism can misguide you in dangerous ways. It may cause you to feel that life is just something that happens to you. This tendency will keep you from uniting your actions with your deepest intentions. In this way it will block you from participating in your own and others' well-being. But the gravest, most pervasive flaw of nihilism is that it will impede awe, appreciation, and the practice of faithing.

In essence, nihilism comes from the inability to reconcile the fathomless nature of things with the efficacy of cause and effect. Yes, you can deny the import of cause and effect all you want, but it won't correspond with your experience of how much things matter to you. Given that this is the case, the way in which we all navigate the world of relationship has deep significance for us. And when I say "us," I strongly suspect this includes most nihilists too.

THE VIEWLESS VIEW

I prostrate to he who has abandoned all views.

—Nagarjuna

The renowned contemporary Buddhist teacher Chögyam Trungpa Rinpoche pointed out the irony inherent in our tendency toward dualism when he said: "The bad news is you're falling through the air, nothing to hang on to, no parachute. The good news is there's no ground." You may misinterpret this to mean that as you confront the truth of emptiness you will always feel like you are falling through space—so you'd better just get used to it. But I don't think this is what Trungpa meant here. I hear him, in the spirit of the Buddha and Nagarjuna, playfully poking fun at our tendencies toward the extremes of eternalism (clinging to existence) and nihilism (fear of extinction), both of which express our inability to rest in the infinite nature of contingent expression.

We have seen for ourselves that things are ultimately unfindable upon investigation, but this doesn't negate the power and splendor of apparent arising. That things are empty of intrinsic characteristics or meaning doesn't leave you all alone to forge your way through a bleak and unfriendly reality. Look around you: you are part of something much, much bigger. When you wake up in the morning each and every day and place your feet on the ground, it is there to support the weight of your body as it always has been. The forces of gravity have never failed to secure your connection to the earth, which keeps you from drifting off into space. How can you not marvel at that?

The topic under discussion in this book, pratityasamutpada, is very "down-to-earth," so to speak, in that you can observe the way it works the minute you wake up and get out of bed each morning. In fact, interdependence functions even in your dreams, reflecting images of your day, your hopes and fears, and the world you are familiar with. The nature of pratityasamutpada has such power that even if you wanted to get rid of the ground you stand on—even if you ripped out the flooring and foundation of your house and tried to dig away the earth beneath it—you would always find a place to put your feet.

The purpose of the investigations we have explored have one aim: to liberate you from the limits of dualism, such as belief and doubt, eternalism and nihilism, ground and groundlessness. But it is also worthy to note that our dualistic struggle for security—although founded on ignorance—reflects a noble intention: we are all simply looking for a place of ease, a refuge. The problem is that there is nothing that makes you more vulnerable to pain, loss, confusion, or disappointment than clinging to ground in a world in which everything leans.

Trying to imagine a life beyond ground and groundlessness can be a philosophical stumper for the dualistic mind, which is precisely why we keep turning to direct experience as our method of exploration in this book. Whenever you feel lost or groundless, recall a moment of grace—a time when you felt completely free and at ease. You might compare this natural ease to returning home after a long, arduous journey. Perhaps grace has, in moments, felt so familiar to you that you may have even wondered if you had ever actually left it. Such experiences may often come upon you by surprise, but they also might be something you want to pay attention to and seek out. You may wonder, "How do I continue to return to grace? How do I find this natural resting place? And is it possible to never part from it?"

The Buddha lived in grace. What this means is that he experienced freedom from the insecurities that accompany extreme views. We usually think of views as conceptual beliefs. But the term *views* here also includes the deep-rooted emotional tendencies we have to cling to existence and nonexistence or ground and groundlessness. In the *Heart Sutra*, buddhas are described by Avalokiteshvara as having "gone, gone, gone beyond, gone completely beyond." You may wonder, "Beyond what?"—all eternalistic and nihilistic views.

To go "beyond views" here refers to the insight of the Middle Way. The Middle Way does not refer to moderation or compromise; it does not represent a mixing together of eternalism and nihilism or a balance of spirituality with worldly life. Neither is it a state of mind or spiritual realm one retreats to. The Middle Way refers to what the Buddha experienced when everything extraneous to the nature—all the extreme views—falls away and one sees the naked truth, unimpeded by one's own misunderstandings. As the great scholar Shantideva said that when "thing" and "non-thing" both indeed are absent from before the mind, nothing else remains for mind to do but rest in perfect peace, free from concepts.[2]

Shantideva's statement clarifies a crucial point: The Middle Way is not yet another view to cling to. It is a way of being that expresses humility and openness, in which there is no trace of affirmation or denial. It was from this place of unshakable confidence that the Buddha, in what is known in the Buddhist tradition as a lion's roar, made a proclamation of resolute fearlessness that comes from discovering the naked truth as a living experience. He said to his close disciple Katyayana, "That things exist is one extreme. That they do not exist is another. But I, the Tathagata, accept neither 'is' or 'is not,' and I declare the truth from the Middle Position."[3]

The Buddha's lion's roar emphasizes the ease, composure, and confidence that accompany resting in the Middle Way of being. You may be able to understand this kind of confidence simply by recalling the moments of grace you have experienced. To be able to

tolerate the magnificence of the nature of emptiness without clinging to existence and nonexistence is what we have been referring
to as faithing. In this way, you might have already begun to draw a
correlation between faithing and *Middle Way-ing*.

Yes, we could also add an *-ing* to the Middle Way if we so choose.
Both faithing and Middle Waying refer to a path and a way of abid-
ing or being in life. They both demand openness, humility, and a
fierce refusal to collapse into ordinary dualistic thinking. They are
for those who understand that life is not a mystery to be solved, for
those who instead have an allegiance to awe and the wisdom that
thoroughly enjoys the magical expression of interdependent arising.
Bringing together faith and the Middle Way has been my challenge
and vision in writing this book.

Faith is a personal and direct experience that you can only define
for yourself. But it is also a shared experience—a conversation—we
humans have had with each other throughout history as we have
participated in life together through language. In light of this, I
thought it would be of tremendous value to bring the wisdom of
pratityasamutpada into the bigger conversation regarding faith.

I don't know of any other path to faithing that uses the unique
and practical methodology of pratityasamutpada. At the same time,
by saying this I don't mean to imply that the true spirit of this tradition differs in essence from the profound and original wisdom of all
the great faith traditions. Like I said before, I think the origin of all
these great lineages was grounded in experiences of emptiness long
before their later adherents could no longer bear the brilliance of
the naked truth and withdrew into rightness or doubt. Our ability to
faith, to appreciate the nature of interdependence, to look at things
with awe and humility is not the turf of any one tradition. It belongs
to us all in that it is nothing more than discovering who we truly are.

4

Citizenship

PERFECT

Even though we live in such an imperfect world, we have a
notion of absolute perfection and completeness.

—Karen Armstrong, *The Case for God*

Have you ever noticed that you move back and forth between what
can seem like parallel universes? Do you ever have an experience
when, one moment, you feel absolutely no hope for humanity;
then in the next you see someone do something completely selfless,
brilliant, and daring, and all of a sudden you feel overcome by the
beauty of it all, and everything seems perfect?

You might keep these experiences to yourself, because in certain
contexts, expressing the opinion that "everything is perfect" could
make people wonder what planet you live on. After all, from one
perspective, when has the world ever been perfect? We are all subject to old age, sickness, and death. War, destruction, abuse, trauma,
and natural disasters seem integral to the human experience. Even
when you sit quietly to meditate, you may, at times, feel bombarded
by the jaggedness of your thoughts and emotions—as if you were
being attacked by your own mind. An unsettled mind feels far from
perfect. This is not to say that you can't find plenty of beauty and
wellness in the world, but my point here is that sometimes saying

that things are perfect can sound a lot like you are living in a deep state of denial.

I want to make a case for perfect as a way of talking about the experience of grace. The term *perfect* in this context does not refer to seeing things as sublime as opposed to ordinary or desirable as opposed to undesirable. It is not a dismissal of suffering or an attempt to live around the challenges we all face. And it is not a philosophy through which to view the world. Perfect does not take place in the dualistic world of our preferences. Rather, perfect reveals itself to us only when we step outside the system of dualism altogether. What I am trying to get at here is that perfect belongs to the mind in awe of its fathomless universe.

You may appreciate moments of awe but think that such experiences have no practical purpose amid the gritty realities of your daily life, where you are often forced to confront serious decisions and focus most of your attention on the work you need to do in order to sustain your basic needs. This assumption is something I want to ask you to reconsider, because awe does indeed have a specific function in our lives. In life, awe is fundamentally linked to our sense of well-being. As we have discussed at length, disturbing emotions arise only when we have already decided what something is—when we fail to look at people or situations as part of the play of mutual causality. More specifically, awe serves as a protection from fundamentalism, rightness, and despair.

When we deprive the mind of openness and curiosity, even our noblest attempts to effect change become militaristic and righteous. We might helicopter into a situation in order to save the day, with a strong conviction that we know what's going on and how to fix it. But when all of our ideas and activities congregate around the truth of our hypothesis, it won't even occur to us that others may have something to offer or that there is something we ourselves can learn. This is when even good intentions express themselves as rigid forms of political correctness or when a vow, which is intended to open up an inquiry, becomes something limited by shoulds and shouldn'ts. Reification gives way to reactivity and deprives us of a sense of awe, and we lose our ability to respond with clarity, efficacy, and tenderness.

Another iteration of rightness becomes apparent when we fail in our attempt to effect change—at least in the way that we want to see it—and find ourselves collapsing under the weight of our own hopes and fears. In realizing that the world is not something we can resolve, we give up. There is no awe in this approach either. Why? Because, yet again, we have decided we know how things are, and this time we conclude that they are hopeless. At a teaching I attended, Joanna Macy gave some advice to a sincere young woman who asked her, with tears streaming down her face, how to work with the despair she felt regarding environmental degradation. Macy gave an unexpected reply; she said, "You wouldn't want to be devoid of the capacity to feel unpleasantness, would you?"

What I understood Macy to be saying is that it is only through our ability to let life touch us that we can awaken to the fullness of our human potential and our ability to respond to the world with accurate empathy. After all, life demands a bit of heartbreak, doesn't it? A tender heart has unlimited give—it can accommodate the full spectrum of sentient experience. If we allow our heart to continuously break as a practice, we will make space for the infinite suffering and beauty of our world, excluding nothing and no one. So why not let it break?

What happens when we expose our despair to a little curiosity and awe? In its nonfrozen version (or should I say, *our* nonfrozen perception), despair begins to look a lot like compassion. And as we begin to break free from the stagnation that comes from the assumption that we are right, an effortless flow of unexpected creativity, insight, and natural responsiveness releases. What's not practical about that?

I want to make sure that you understand that the nondual experience of perfect we have been looking at here doesn't come about by turning away from suffering and seeking joy or from trying to forcibly equalize pleasant and unpleasant experiences into a neutral state. Nondual refers to a commitment to value and utilize all experience as a means to awaken. That seems like a tall order, doesn't it? But in a way, we are talking about a simple shift of focus—a way of framing life—where, instead of blaming the world or feeling that life is something that happens *to* you, you decide to see whatever you encounter as an opportunity and privilege. You choose to own it with a sense of pride.

Using all experience as an opportunity to grow doesn't mean that you should view all unwanted circumstances as your fault—not at all. In fact, you might look at owning challenges as an empowerment of sorts. I have noticed for myself a slight feeling of irreverence and a burst of defiant energy when I say, "Ha-ha, this challenge is mine now." In other words, when you decide to own it, you no longer give undue power to external circumstances. If you think about it, that would be giving truth to an object that it never actually possessed in the first place—in other words, this thing was never a singular, permanent, or independent reality.

The commitment to value everything presents us with a way out of victimhood and is the ultimate support for growth and healing. It is not just an attitude, but requires the insight that is able to see through delusion. After all, how can you take on a challenging experience if you don't understand that it does not—by its very nature—exist as it appears? Again, we find ourselves returning to the essential insight we have been exploring in this book: because everything leans, things do not possess intrinsic characteristics from their own side and hence cannot be known in a determinate way.

We often claim to be open-minded, but the moment we shut down around an object and decide what it is, we succumb to fundamentalism and rightness. Fundamentalism is simply the inability to bear the fathomless nature of things. Why not affectionately call that "mind at its worst." There is no need to be hard on yourself about your tendency to reify things; it is a challenge that comes with being human. Have a bit of curiosity about this tendency, and learn how it operates, because the way in which we close down around an object—or not—is directly linked to moving in and out of grace.

We are capable of great despair, confusion, and ugliness. But we are also capable of moving through life with grace. We are trying to find our place within the great nature of interdependent expression, which we could call "mind at its best." In a sense, you might say that we are learning to respect our self, others, and the world we move about in. And the greatest respect we could possibly have for anyone (or anything) is to not assume we know who anyone is.

BURNING WITH LOVE IN A WORLD WE CAN'T FIX

Our endeavor is not religious, but rather a test of what we as a human being can become, the greatest unfolding of our potential.

—Dzigar Kongtrul Rinpoche

Because everything leans, you belong to something much, much greater than what you may often refer to as "the world" or "my life"; you belong to something greater than your community, political party, nation, or even this magnificent planet Earth. You are a noble citizen of the boundless field of contingent relationships, pratityasamutpada.

I suspect that you naturally sense a connection to something bigger than the ordinary responsibilities and concerns of your daily life, but you may forget this at times. When you awaken to it, however, a fierce tenderness might arise in you, along with a deep longing to reach out to others: sometimes with a sense of urgency, sometimes with the spirit of playfulness, always with a deep sense of caring. This kind of responsiveness is not a matter of principle; it is a matter of the heart. You could call it love, but the idea of love is already a bit formed, whereas responsiveness describes the step before love becomes an idea, which is very natural, unconditional, and raw.

Although you may, at times, brace against life, it is not possible to withdraw from the nature of interdependent expression. You could hide yourself in a cave and block the entrance with a massive boulder, but you would still need the ground to support the weight of your body; you would still breathe in the air of that small space and feel its temperature on your skin; and, of course, the natural vitality of thoughts and emotions would continue to express themselves in the field of your awareness, based upon memories and imprints you have taken in through your senses. You will never be able to say where you as an individual end and the world begins, as you are neither the same nor separate from the world around you. You really are a citizen of this infinite place, and the more you are able to move out of contraction, the more you will feel the poignancy and value of contingent relationship. After all, grace doesn't happen in a vacuum.

In the classical Indian Buddhist text *The Way of the Bodhisattva*, Shantideva uses a unique analogy to talk about how our relationship to others motivates responsiveness. He says that just as your limbs extend outward from the trunk of your own body, you could include all conscious creatures as extensions of your ever-expanding self. In other words, you could make the world your body.[1] Something is brewing here: I do believe Shantideva is introducing us to a plan of action. And it is timely, because to look honestly at our place in the nature of pratityasamutpada as we have been doing thus far has provided us with a realistic and intelligent working basis or ground for creating grace. But this alone will not be enough. We will need some infrastructure to support awakening. Let's call this the path.

There are many genuine spiritual paths. And they all show us how to utilize the phenomenal world to create grace. The tradition of the Buddhist Mahayana, which is the tradition associated with the teachings on pratityasamutpada, presents us with a plan for awakening, and it is phrased in a most provocative and curious way: "Beings are limitless, I vow to free them all." Just in case this commitment sounds a bit overwhelming, I want to say that it is not meant to corner you into anything, but rather to help hold you in the boundary of your intention to find grace in relationship. You might even look at it as a proposal or an invitation that, if taken to heart, will provide you with a poignant directive for your life.

At first glance you might find this proposal a bit cryptic. You might struggle with its whole premise. Many people do. It may even sound a bit arrogant to you. You may argue: "All the great sages throughout history have been unable to take away the suffering of others, so who am I to do it?" You may also question what it would mean to free someone, given that freedom is something everyone must find within herself or himself. Furthermore, this vow doesn't necessarily make sense within the framework of ordinary logic. "After all," you may wonder, "if beings are limitless, suffering is also limitless, so how could one possibly free them all?" Indeed, this is an impossible task.

Yet when you bear witness to the suffering in the world around you, how can you resist the urge to do something? And as you begin to reach out, you may naturally discover that the vow to free all beings is asking you to do something unexpected, remarkable, and within your reach. It invites you to move outside the barriers of ordinary logic and enter into a different way of seeing things. Try to frame it in this way: "Yes, beings are limitless, and their suffering is also limitless, so I will have to expand the realm of my care limitlessly, in order to include them all." The mind set on this aspiration transforms the vow to serve all beings into a living practice. If you possess the fortitude for living in the heart of such a challenge, the practice of *bodhichitta* may interest you.

Bodhichitta is a Sanskrit word: *bodhi* means "awakened," and *chitta* refers to both "mind" and "heart." In other words, the Sanskrit term *chitta* does not separate heartfelt responsiveness from the clarity of discerning insight. When one sees the nature of interdependence clearly, one naturally responds to the world with tenderness and care, knowing that because everything leans, everything we do matters. Yet bodhichitta is not just a crusade to do good. Naturally, it is motivated by love and care, but as we have discussed and come to understand, things are unfindable. So it follows that, although our actions can and do influence or interrupt the flow of things, this world of ours is not some singular, permanent, or independent thing we can resolve, secure, or bring to a static state of peaceful equilibrium. On one hand we feel compelled to reach out; on the other, we must bear witness to the fathomless and unfixable nature of things.

Those who live in the heart of this gorgeous conundrum are called bodhisattvas. You could describe a bodhisattva as one who burns with love while knowing that the world itself is not something that can be resolved. The bodhisattva isn't unsettled or daunted by insight into the unfixable nature of things, not at all. This very insight is the wellspring of responsiveness. Driven by insight, the question continually haunts bodhisattvas: "How can I serve?" This is a beautiful way to live.

Service can take shape in grand gestures, if such opportunities arise. But quiet gestures can be just as powerful: placing a loving hand on someone's shoulder as a reminder that he or she is not alone; rescuing a small insect from a pool of water; or warmly inviting someone to "jump in!" your lane during that busy time at the swimming pool. Such actions are never prescribed, which frees the bodhisattva to respond with accurate empathy. The joy that comes from reaching out to others in this way sustains the path of the bodhisattva without any question as to how one might bring spiritual practice into one's daily life. The bodhisattva just keeps the question open: "How can I serve?" The bodhisattva plays fiercely within the world of phenomena, despite the unfixable nature of life, as the ultimate skillful means to awaken both oneself and others.

That the world is not resolvable might raise some questions for you about the way in which you typically understand evolution. Most people generally think of evolution as linear progress: a promise that life will get better, that we as a species will continue to increase our intelligence and invent more sophisticated technologies that will somehow resolve the human condition. But when we look at the nature of infinite contingency, we see that, in fact, the world is not moving in a smooth or linear direction, and it is not necessarily getting better.

In the tradition of pratityasamutpada, the scriptures describe our typical condition in life as like a bee in a jar. Sometimes the bee circles the top of the jar, and at other times it circles the bottom. In the same way, we most likely make some progress in our jar, which metaphorically speaking refers to those times we find ourselves circling the top—getting what we want. We may get promoted at work, take a trip to the moon, or invent a new vaccine; we may experience some real victories, in fact. Yet we cannot avoid also not getting what we want or getting what we don't want, confusion, loss, and then death, of course. I don't think we can genuinely call this evolution. In fact, in the Buddhist world, this is called *samsara*, which literally means "going around and around in circles."

Striving for linear progress does not solve the predicaments of living beings, not at all. However, evolution in the context of the nature of pratityasamutpada is entirely different. It is the process of emancipating ourselves from the jar of delusion altogether, which can be momentary, or it can be a place that we eventually live in. The path of bodhichitta—which is embodied in the full execution of the vow itself—provides us with the infrastructure to do just this. And it is our job to bring it all to life: to find our place in the nature of infinite contingency and in doing so fiercely serve all beings.

CHOICE

We live within movements constantly affecting each other and creating an unpredictable chaos at many levels. Yet within this same chaos is born all the physical and psychological order that we know.

—F. David Peat

You might wonder, as you pursue the path of bodhichitta, how much choice do you actually have? What are the limitations and freedoms of the nature of pratityasamutpada, and how can you harness them in order to make a positive difference within its boundaryless field of expression?

These questions relate to the creative aspect of dependent arising and how you are to move about in it. The activity of dependent arising is often known by the Sanskrit term *karma* and commonly translated as "activity." Because everything leans, karma expresses itself as a whole lot of energy and movement. The late contemporary Buddhist teacher Traleg Rinpoche, in his book *Karma*, explains how critical it is to explore the power and efficacy of karma. But he also explains that "karma is not altogether un-mysterious either because the level of the complexity of interrelatedness has to be appreciated."[2]

In other words, the vast working of karma can't be known in its entirety, because the open-dimensional nature of things is not limited to the way in which you perceive them. Yet that doesn't mean you can't clearly identify patterns and causal relationships. Human beings and animals both most certainly can and do. And based upon this ability to observe how things work, we have figured out how to survive in the world: metaphorically and literally—how to plant a seed and reap the fruit.

There is no denying that an apple seed (given the necessary causes and conditions) will share a continuum with an apple tree and not a banana tree. The nature of pratityasamutpada expresses itself with absolute precision and integrity. So while upon analysis things are unfindable, in this tradition there is no argument with the way things appear to function. If you were to approach a farmer and try to explain to him that if he observed the process carefully, he wouldn't be able to find the moment an apple shoot emerged from its seed, he would ask you where you planned on getting your produce.

Even during times when the world looks like sheer mayhem, your very ability to effect change and get things done provides evidence enough that karma is at work. What you might often interpret as arbitrary is just your own inability to identify patterns in a way that makes sense to you. But just consider this: from the chaotic appearance of a brewing storm falls a perfectly symmetrical snowflake. So although you can't find linear causation upon examination, it doesn't mean there is not an intricacy and efficacy to karma that at times you just cannot see.

Of course, while pondering that snowflake, you might begin to look for a hidden blueprint or singular cause behind its perfect symmetry. When we recognize harmony in relationships—often with things we consider to be of great beauty—it is not unusual for us to attribute their source to a singular, eternal organizing principle. But upon investigation, we were unable to find a singular source for creation, and this naturally redirected us back, yet again, to the nature of mutual dependency.

Mutual causation is an open system, wherein everything influences everything else. And this means that although we can infer what might happen next based on previous experience, the magnificent dance of infinite complexity will never be totally predictive. And this means that you have choice within this order and are not completely chained to some kind of cosmic design. Even our genetic dispositions are susceptible to all kinds of surprises that influence the flow of natural systems.

In short, to live within the infinite nature of contingency means that, yes, there is unlimited potential, but if the causes and conditions do not come together for something to happen, it will not happen. For instance, if you jump off a building, you won't be able to fly—simply because you don't have wings—but you can learn to paraglide or fly a plane. You can't force someone into loving you, but you can find unconditional love and deep contentment within yourself, which profoundly opens up your ability to love everyone, and this can sustain you. You can't push the world into a static state of peaceful equilibrium, but your actions (in both big and small ways) will always have reverberating effects, so you can't help but influence the course of history. That's a whole lot of power and choice.

Whether we make a conscious choice to follow a lineage of wisdom or not, it has always been our natural inclination to bend toward well-being. You might say that you have always been searching for grace. Our search expresses itself the moment we are born into life and instinctively cry out to suckle and find comfort in our mother's arms. From there, we have so much to learn, which requires lots of playful experimentation—and I mean play in a broad sense: how we interact with life, how we influence it, how it shapes us, and how we figure out how to bring our actions together with our intentions.

As children we are all driven by a natural curiosity. I suspect, like most children, you did things you were told not to do in order to see for yourself how things worked, like touching a hot stove with your finger or sticking your tongue out at your neighbor. The pressure to not do what you were told made the doing all the more tantalizing, and the consequences of such doings became part of this playful experimentation too. There is a daring and curiosity in this type of play, from which we all learn about the ways of the world, about the nature of the physical elements and the feedback we get from challenging behavioral agreements found in any given social context.

Throughout our adult life play continues. The ongoing exchange you have with life takes place all the time: the cold air touches your skin, so you put on a sweater. After you put on your cozy sweater you step outside. Let's say you get into your car, put the key in the ignition, and turn it. The engine begins to rumble. After a few minutes on the road you might arrive at an intersection, where you stop at a stop sign. You stop because you share an agreement with other drivers and pedestrians to follow the rules of the road and respect civic infrastructure. You may sometimes resent having to work within the boundaries of these kinds of restrictions, but in fact, such systems help direct your life in a positive way, by helping you get to where you want to go safely. I wouldn't dismiss rules or laws as lying outside the nature of play. They are creative constructs that harness the nature of cause and effect to bring about specific results.

All day long you bump up against things, provoke, push, yield to, finesse, and flirt with the many possibilities you are able to perceive. Sometimes you fail to align your actions with your intentions, and other times you succeed. Sometimes you hurt people. Sometimes they hurt you. At times you have a glimmer of seeing the world as being unconditionally perfect. "Where do such experiences come from," you might wonder, "and why do they come and go?" These were the types of questions the Buddha asked himself on his way to awakening from delusion. He relentlessly engaged in playful experimentation until he played his way into grace. This is how he discovered the path of awakening.

5

Living Tradition

To help you on this path, you have the maps left by the buddhas, bodhisattvas, teachers, and lineage masters of the past.
What did they encounter on their journey . . . what did or
did not work for them? Due to their kindness, you have this
incredible information to use and enjoy.

—Dzigar Kongtrul Rinpoche, *It's Up to You*

History reveals that humans have always used form and ritual to
invoke protection from the powerful forces of nature and to mark
important transitions, such as rites of passage from childhood into
adulthood and from life to death. Across both culture and time we
have used purification rituals as a way of processing the pain of re-
morse; consecration ceremonies for initiating places and objects
with significant functions; and music, poetry, and art to creatively
express and acknowledge visible outward and inward experiences
of grace. Some of these traditions have been passed down with great
tenderness and purpose for thousands of generations.

The renowned Indian Buddhist teacher Asanga describes the
spiritual path as having two aspects: scripture and realization.
Realization refers to the authentic continuum of living wisdom
passed down through a succession of accomplished scholars and

meditators, insight that words can't capture. Scripture refers to the forms, ritual, and language used to carry a tradition forward in order to evoke and honor realization and the experience of grace. It describes how we utilize the phenomenal world with specificity and deliberation, to hold us within the boundaries of our intention to evolve as human beings.

One of the most valued and widely recited texts in the Buddhist tradition, the *Heart Sutra* helps elucidate the relationship between scripture and realization. In some versions, the sutra begins with an introduction that describes the scenario in which the Buddha taught the sutra for the first time. On the top of a hill perched above an expansive valley in northern India known as Vulture Peak, an assembly of ordained practitioners and bodhisattvas gather around the Buddha, riveted with anticipation, to receive his teachings. Curiously, throughout most of the sutra, the Buddha sits silently in meditation as a way of illustrating that insight can't be captured in words or known through ordinary concepts.

At the same time, the bodhisattva Avalokiteshvara serves as the Buddha's mouthpiece, describing the insight of emptiness in words that constitute the sutra itself. It is not until the very end that the Buddha praises the words of Avalokiteshvara, with enthusiasm—"Thus it is, thus it is!"—reminding us that the illusory tools of language and communication do not function as truths but rather as means that open us to grace. As the path unfolds, one begins to grasp the powerful function and sacredness of words and gestures that constitute tradition.

In most spiritual traditions you find both highly ritualized forms of worship and hermetic practices that foster silence and solitude. But observers use rituals, even in their most stripped-down guises, as a way of including the sensual world in the realm of spiritual discovery. Ritual creates a container for transformation to take place. Even the ascetic practices of wearing rough burlap robes or fasting, for instance, utilize humble manifestations of form as a way of exploring the sensual world of unconditional richness. We might think of the forms and rituals we use as tools to evoke insight, to appreciate the world of appearance, and to create grace.

In truth, our lives are full of ritual: handshaking, jury trials, executions, political elections, birthday parties, weddings, and funerals. Rising to pledge allegiance to a national flag or to cheer for your favorite football team is a gesture of reverence and thus a kind of ritual. Even waking up in the morning to perform your daily ablutions and make coffee are among the countless rituals we perform as individuals and societies each day. There is no way of living without ritual, yet we often assume that we either have to buy into rituals or else rebel against them. Due to the limiting nature of this very assumption, the topic of tradition and ritual deserves consideration.

Whether in a spiritual or mundane context, subtle shoulds and shouldn'ts creep in that make forms feel rigid, archaic, and impersonal. We refer to spiritual communities by the somewhat derogatory term organized religion when they feel entrenched with prescribed beliefs or we feel a lack of personal connection to their purpose. Spirituality stagnates when it becomes a closed system.

The theoretical physicist F. David Peat talks about closed systems as "limit cycles." You will often find limit cycles in collective belief systems, such as *organized religions* or political parties, when individuals cling to rightness or truth in forms and ideas. Codependent relationships that enable neurotic behavior in families also entail clinging to an unhealthy dynamic, for instance, around an addiction. Sometimes you might take on another person's limit cycle in the form of a belief. An example of a limit cycle, in your own experience, might be a way in which you devote your internal energy to resisting change.

In contrast, we can observe in nature that the more open a species is to a variety of habitats, the more vital it is. And the more restricted a species is to a narrow, particular set of conditions, the more vulnerable it becomes to the inevitable change that will at some point sweep through that habitat. No habitat remains stagnant. Sooner or later, enough of a change occurs to upset the inhabitants.

As we have discussed, within the nature of interdependent relationships there is no such thing as a closed system, so trying to resist change requires a lot of contraction, a stubborn refusal to let life touch you, and a rigorous attempt to rearrange the world according to your preferences. In a limit cycle there is no sense of collaborating with the universe of interdependent relationship, of which you are an integral part.

The illustrious Thich Nhat Hanh, in the first of his fourteen precepts of engaged Buddhism, taught: "Do not be idolatrous about or bound to any doctrine, theory, or ideology, even Buddhist ones. Buddhist systems of thought are guiding means; they are not absolute truth."[1] This is such a freeing Middle Way statement. Please don't misunderstand it, though, as a rejection of traditional practice and ideas.

You may find in yourself a tendency to harbor suspicion toward traditional ideas and practices that seem dry and that challenge your sense of freethinking. At a time when scientific knowledge has become the arbiter of truth, you may dismiss formal practices of ritual as archaic, foreign, or even embarrassing in a world where engaging such things is seen as simpleminded and naive. When you let your practice dry up or allow others to define it for you, you may complain that the path isn't working and try to create something new. You may think, "After all, we are Americans; let's create a new American Buddhism."

I like the adventurous spirit and creativity of Americans, but with that spirit often comes the danger of customized spirituality. We customize spirituality by replacing that which feels uncomfortable with a brand of spirituality that provides comfort but little transformation. We may attempt to tease out authentic bits of wisdom— the ones that make you feel good—from the rest of a tradition or dismiss an entire tradition altogether. An example of this would be to dismiss the word *faith* rather than looking more deeply at its etymology, at its wide range of meaning, and at how you personally experience it.

To inquire opens a window into transformation, and we need to really ask ourselves if that is what we want: Do you really want to change? Or do you feel set on staying the way you are and holding on to your beliefs, even if they are based on rejection of a wisdom tradition? How could such an approach serve you? A path that aims at living around life can lead only to a watered-down version of anything. Rejecting forms, it turns out, is really just the other side of holding on to them—just another limit cycle based on the stubborn refusal to soften the boundaries of your truths.

The tendency to bail in the face of discomfort is just the other side of holding on to views. However, if the pursuit of grace inspires you, you have to be willing to poke just a little hole in your truths, to investigate them just a bit to see what you may find. Transformation cannot take place if you jump from one thing to another, because, as it turns out, there is nothing you can ever engage that always brings contentment and comfort. To understand this is to dispel the myth of exit freedom: the assumption that it is the world outside that binds you, that liberation comes from fleeing whenever the going gets rough. Of course, we never find authentic freedom this way because, as they say, "wherever you go, there you are." Grace, as we have discussed, comes from uniting discernment together with openness and humility.

I once heard a Buddhist teacher say that the whole point of having a teacher was to become autonomous. I considered that for a while. I thought, "Well, yes, as a mother, I did everything I could to help my son stand on his own two feet. I get that." But is it possible for anyone to stand on their own two feet without their mother, father, or guardian to guide them? When we are born, we are completely helpless and dependent. We would never survive without the help of others. There is truly no such thing as autonomy. So if you want to live in accordance with the nature of things—which means living in grace—practically speaking, it will require some humility and gratitude for the ways in which your tradition has come down to you with so much care.

In contemporary culture we often equate humility with weakness, submission, or stupidity. But the nature of pratityasamutpada, as we have been discussing it throughout this book, leads us to understanding that humility comes from a deep appreciation of who we are in the context of a universe in which everything leans. Living in accord with the way things are empowers us. And we need to feel empowered because, in truth, it is our task to keep the inquiry alive and not fall into spiritual vagueness. No one else, not even the teacher, can ultimately do this for us.

Please don't misunderstand me here. I am not necessarily trying to make a pitch for organized religion. I am only asking you to question whether either buying into forms or dismissing them are your only options. Of course, as we have also been discussing throughout this book, there is the Middle Way that takes us beyond belief and doubt, beyond grasping and rejection. Middle Waying or faithing is the process of open inquiry that brings it all to life in the most personal way. This is traditional Buddhism and, it seems to me, the essence of all authentic spiritual traditions.

It excites and sometimes concerns me to witness the timeless wisdom of the Buddhist tradition enter into the wild, cocky, and creative atmosphere of contemporary culture. I wonder if it will endure the test of time. Well, that will depend upon whether those who practice it maintain the spirit of open inquiry. This is a very personal question for each of us.

THE LOGIC OF FAITH

It is vital for us to obtain genuine confidence in the nature of mind and reality, grounded in understanding and reason.

—His Holiness the Fourteenth Dalai Lama

Logic is thought to belong solely to the realm of the intellect: a + b = c. Numerical systems, theories, and language only work within the confines of man-made arbitrary systems but cannot describe the liveliness of the world in which we live.

But in this book, we have taken a different approach to logic. In the spirit and tradition of pratityasamutpada, we have engaged logical discernment in connection with direct experience. We have brought together our natural gift of discernment with an attitude of complete openness, which has allowed us to perceive our object (everything and anything) without the impediments that come with shutting down around conceptual truths. Genuine insight and confidence reveal themselves only to a mind that can withstand the brilliance and fathomless nature of interdependence, without clinging to definitive notions of is and is not. The act of bearing witness to experience in this way I have referred to as faithing.

The logic of faith, as presented here, can be understood in a simple statement: because everything leans, nothing exists in a definitive way. So it follows that the only way to know without error comes with the insight that does not seek determinate truths.

As Joanna Macy so astutely puts it:

> From the viewpoint of mutual causality the impossibility of arriving at ultimate definitions and formulations of reality does not represent a defeat for the inquiring mind. It is only final assertions that are suspect, not the process of knowing itself.[2]

This is a logical deduction, but one that can only be understood directly, through examining your own experience. Through understanding, conviction takes root. We find in the study of pratityasamutpada a different way of knowing that goes beyond the limits of is and is not. In light of this, it is my hope that you have discovered, through the investigations presented in this book, that there is no need to abandon logic in order to faith.

When you take up the task of your own awakening through direct investigation, it gives spirituality traction in the context of your day-to-day life. We cannot expect spiritual transcendence while entrenched in the realm of fixed ideas and vague assumptions. Without bringing awareness to the light of our direct experience, spirituality becomes yet another egoic enterprise based on cherishing and protecting abstract notions of self. You may find that in the context of your own path you hold on more than you let go and that even after years of meditation, prayer, and belief you have yet to do the work of letting in life. This is something important to continually check: what actually is the purpose of a spiritual path?

You might reply, "To alleviate suffering." Yes, it is reasonable to want out of suffering. But in the context of a universe in which everything leans, is it possible to arrive at a perfect state of peaceful equilibrium, where you no longer have to feel the pain and challenges of the human condition? Furthermore, is this what you really want?

My teacher has often said that the Middle Way path is not about seeking peace. Seeking peace entails a search for preferred experiences, where one evaluates and separates life by way of what one does or doesn't want. The path of pratityasamutpada offers something bolder and more enlivening. It challenges you to bear the mystery rather than seeking conclusions, to let life touch you rather than trying to live around it, to analyze the nature of things rather than shutting down around coarse ideas and dogmas. It encourages you to explore these so-called things that you keep shrinking from and reacting to. Is it possible to let yourself feel the full range of human experience—life—without shutting down or chasing after it?

The authentic practice of pratityasamutpada, it turns out, offers a path for being big enough for your life. It teaches us that there is a happiness that does not exclude suffering, that does not require you keep the fullness of life at bay. And you can let in all that life when you understand that things are not limited to the assumptions you have about them. This is where the teachings of pratityasamutpada come in and challenge your notions of realness.

Since the momentous day I sat with my teacher on that hill in Nepal, I have come to understand the potency and power of his simple gesture. By pressing his two index fingers together, he was giving me my first instructions on pratityasamutpada, showing me that everything leans. It is easy to underestimate the power and sophistication of this essential teaching. Please know that insight into interdependence lies at the very core of the Buddha's realization and path. Such insight is interruptive to our tenacious systems of delusion.

As I clearly see my teacher's gesture in my mind's eye, it reminds me that I am not one, nor am I two; I am not the same, nor am I separate from the fathomless nature of interdependent expression. I am not in total command, yet everything I do matters. I am neither big nor small. I am, however, part of the great nature of infinite contingency, and in the moments I embody this wisdom, I live in grace. And even in the times my habitual tendencies overwhelm me and I let the appearance of things outshine their nature, I have faith in the nature of interdependence and the path of pratityasamutpada. Having seen this, there is no going back. It has become an obvious truth.

I wrote this book as a tribute to the experience of grace, the source from which all authentic faith traditions have emerged. But I also had something else in mind. I wanted to introduce the tradition of pratityasamutpada into a bigger conversation regarding faith. I wanted to present an investigation that would liberate faith from the stagnant realm of individual and cultural beliefs and go beyond the vague assumptions that remain locked up in language. I wanted to bring to the fore the practice of faithing or Middle Waying as protection from the extremes of eternalism and nihilism that run rampant in these times of extreme fundamentalism and doubt.

As I write the final chapter of this book, I continue to delight in the exploration of this single word—*faith*—and to the process of opening into inexhaustible universes rich with information and insight. I have used phrases and terms to point to the experience of faith, drawing on both personal examples and cultural narratives. Yet, as colorful, playful, and descriptive as these words may be, language always falls short of the liveliness of a direct experience.

So though it's said that all things must come to an end, I would have to disagree with that statement. In fact, I believe it's an expression that's in need of some serious reexamination! Within the responsive nature of interdependent expression, every thing influences every other thing. And that means life will always be a work in progress. So although this book reaches its final pages, who can predict what will come from it? Writing it undoubtedly changed the way I see things. My hope is that it will keep you interested so that you never shut down around words and experiences or fall into fundamentalism and doubt, to see that unconditional confidence does not come from clinging to views.

I thank you for joining me in reconsidering the word *faith*. It is my hope that you have discovered, through the investigations presented in this book, no need to abandon logic in order to faith. After all, given that the world doesn't lend itself to being known in a determinate way, faithing may very well be the only logical response to living in a world where everything leans.

NOTES

INTRODUCTION: THE F-WORD

1. Thinley Norbu, *Magic Dance* (Boston: Shambhala, 1999), 90.
2. In the Buddhist scriptures you will find the term *pratityasa-mutpada* used in two ways: on a specific level, pratityasamut-pada refers to the application of this general principle in a teaching called the twelve links of dependent arising. We will not explore this teaching explicitly in this book. Rather we will focus on the Buddha's insight into pratityasamutpada in a general way: as the central insight from which all his teach-ings—such as the teachings on karma, suffering, liberation, and emptiness—emerged.

CHAPTER 1: WHAT DO I KNOW?

1. F. David Peat, *From Certainty to Uncertainty: The Story of Sci-ence and Ideas in the Twentieth Century* (Washington, DC: John Henry Press, 2002), 106.
2. Majjhima Nikaya II.32, a Buddhist scripture, the second of the five *nikayas*, or collections, in the *Sutta Pitaka*, which is one of the three baskets that compose the Pali Tipitaka of Theravada Buddhism, composed between the third century B.C.E. and second century C.E. This nikaya consists of 152 discourses attributed to the Buddha and his chief disciples. Here I have used a translation from Joanna Macy's book, *Mutual Causality in Buddhism and General Systems Theory* (Albany, NY: State University of New York Press, 1991), 53.
3. Richard Barron's translation of the Tibetan word *nang-sal*,

a descriptive way of speaking about *all* phenomena, both conscious and material.

CHAPTER 2: INVESTIGATING THINGS

1. Tom O'Brian, "New Clock May End Time As We Know It," *NPR*, November 3, 2014, www.npr.org/2014/11/03/361069820/new-clock-may-end-time-as-we-know-it.
2. Majjhima Nikaya II.32.
3. Macy, *Mutual Causality*, 63.

CHAPTER 3: FAITH

1. Digha Nikaya II.36, from Macy, *Mutual Causality*, 45.
2. Shantideva, *The Way of the Bodhisattva*, Elizabeth Mattis Namgyel's personal translation of chapter 9, verse 34.
3. Majjhima Nikaya I. 65

CHAPTER 4: CITIZENSHIP

1. Shantideva, *The Way of the Bodhisattva*, chapter 8, verse 114.
2. Traleg Kyabgon, *Karma: What It Is, What It Isn't, Why It Matters* (Boston: Shambhala, 2015), 58.

CHAPTER 5: LIVING TRADITION

1. Thich Nhat Hanh, *Interbeing: Fourteen Guidelines for Engaged Buddhism*, revised ed. (Berkeley, CA: Parallax Press, 1993).
2. Macy, *Mutual Causality*, 130.

INDEX

actions
  bodhichitta and, 107–8
  consequences of, 20
  emptiness and, 69
  intention and, 41, 95–96, 111, 112
addiction, substance, 27
affirmation and denial, 49, 57, 62,
  68, 69, 77, 98
agency, 1, 74, 88
aggregates, 44
American Buddhism, 116
analogies and metaphors
  for appearances, traditional
    Buddhist, 24
  bee in jar, 108–9
  boatman carrying boat, 74
  body as world, 106
  daughter of barren woman, 91
  dreams, 24, 25
  elephants bathing, 67–68, 71
  interview process, 9–10
  line on surface of lake, 55–56
  maps, 44, 45, 47, 66, 80
  pie, baking from scratch,
    58–60, 88
  rainbows, 24, 25
  reeds, two bundles of, 15
  water and ice, 70
analysis, etymology of, 40, 47
  analytical meditation, 39–43,
    94–96. *See also* investiga-
    tions

Anam Thubten, 85
anger, 29–31, 63
animals, reality of, 23
  appearance and possibilities
    (Tib. *nang-sal*), 19, 123n3
appearances
  emptiness and, 65, 66, 69
  interdependent nature of, 25
  outshining their nature, 29, 36,
    121
  seeing beyond, 34
appreciation, 13, 73, 74, 78, 96, 118
arising, apparent, 96
Armstrong, Karen. See *Case for
  God, The*
arrogance, intellectual, 84–85
Aryadeva, 33
Asanga, 113
aspirations, 107
assumptions, 9–10, 76, 120
  about open-mindedness, 9
  about ritual, 115
  breaking constraints of, 57
  challenges to, 5–6
  doubt and, 85
  exhausting, 51, 52
  loosening, 40–41, 47
  reservations in questioning, 67
atoms, 45–46
autonomy, 41–42, 43, 58–62, 61,
  65, 75, 81, 117
Avalokiteshvara, 70, 98, 114

awareness, 20, 106
   of body, 36–38, 48
   continuum of, 24
   direct experience and, 120
   grace and, 13
   in investigations, 35–36, 41, 47,
      51–52
   open-dimensionality of, 31
   as permanent self, investigating,
      53
awe
   allegiance to, 99
   as basis of spirituality, 11, 12,
      89
   in daily life, 102–3
   doubt and, 84
   of Middle Way, 57
   nihilism as impediment to, 96
   pratityasamutpada and, 64

Basic Space of Phenomena, The
   (Longchenpa), 66
bearing witness, 41, 49, 107, 119
Beasts of the Southern Wild, 10
beliefs
   bondage of, 80–81
   and doubt, relationship be-
      tween, 75, 83–85
   eternalism and, 94
   identifying, 27–29
   limit cycles and, 115
   "truth" and, 89–91
   uses of term, 77–78
Blue Marble. *See* earth seen from
   space
bodhichitta, 107–9
bodhisattvas, 108, 114
body, physical
   as label, 39
   as object of investigation,
      36–38
   scanning, 48

and self, association with,
   51–52, 57
Bonaventure, Saint, 73
brilliance, 10, 63, 88, 99, 119
Buddha, 70, 114
   awakening of, 3–4
   grace and, 98, 112
   on not holding on to truth, 74
   pratityasamutpada, and, 15,
      64–65, 91, 121
Buddhism, 88, 90, 116, 118. *See
   also* Indian Buddhism; Mahayana; Tibetan Buddhism

Case for God, The (Armstrong), 7,
   76–77, 78, 101
causal relationships, identifying,
   110
causation, singular source of,
   87–88, 89, 93–94, 110–11
cause and effect, 16, 64–65, 93,
   95, 96. *See also* karma
causes and conditions, 31
   appearance and, 25
   for conception, example of,
      60–61
   eternalism and, 88
   karma and, 110, 111
   multiplicity of, 15
   of self, tracing, 81
certainty/certitude, 8, 13–15, 29,
   76–77
Chandrakirti, 42, 91
change
   constancy of, 14, 29, 50
   as continuum, 55
   effecting, 103, 110
   trying to resist, 115–17
chaos, 109, 110
characteristics, 17, 22, 66, 69,
   96–97, 104
clear seeing, 5, 63, 71

clinging, 9, 26, 39, 71, 84, 89, 91, 115
closed systems, 115–16
cognition, 16, 35
commitment
    to free all beings, 106–9
    to value everything, 103–4
communication, 24, 77–78, 89, 114. *See also* language
compassion, 12, 76, 82, 103
concepts, 37, 39, 57, 62–63, 98, 114
confidence, 12, 119
    of Buddha, 98
    from direct experience, 62, 63
    faith and, 73, 75
    false, 31
    in nature of mind, 118
    in pratityasamutpada, 16, 88
    rightness and, 9, 76
    from seeing for oneself, 40
    unconditional, 122
confusion, 4, 28, 104, 109
    about appearance, 29, 30, 36
    from clinging to ground, 97
    doubt and, 83, 85
    of dualistic thinking, 68
    source of, 89
consciousness, 16, 35–36, 61, 87
contingency
    causes and conditions and, 60–61, 62
    infinite nature of, 66, 74, 81, 89, 108, 109, 111, 121
    of relationships, 69–70
continuity, 54
contraction, 26–27, 95–96, 106
creative expression, 11, 24, 103. *See also* expression, interdependent
curiosity, 9, 34
    in analytical meditation, 43

belief and, 80
deprivation of, 102
despair and, 103
doubt and, 84
faith and, 73, 74
natural, 112
reification and, 104–5
spirituality and, 12

Dalai Lama, His Holiness the Fourteenth, 118
dark nights of the soul, 82–83
death, 81, 92, 109
delusion, 42, 67
    basis of, 69
    choosing, 33
    emancipation from, 109
    and illusion, distinction between, 25, 32
    as inaccurate perception, 21
    interrupting, 121
    seeing through, 104
dependent arising. *See* pratityasamutpada
despair, 102, 103, 104–5
devotion, 43, 82
Dickey Lama, 79–80
Dilgo Khyentse Rinpoche, 11–12
direct experience
    and conceptual understanding, connection between, 57, 62–63
    discernment and, 119
    doubting, 57
    importance of, 40–41, 48, 97
    of looking and not finding, 66
    pratityasamutpada and, 4, 16
discernment
    doubting, 31
    faith and, 74
    grace and, 117
    as guide, 49

discernment (*continued*)
  open-mindedness and, 9
  as prajna, 41–42, 46–47
  Two Truths and, 71
discomfort, 2, 47, 83, 117
dogma, 1, 3, 4, 71, 74, 75–76,
    88–89, 120
doubt, 30, 75
  of direct experience, 57
  of discernment, 31
  exploring, 83–86
  faith and, 1, 89
  Middle Way and, 118, 121, 122
  nihilism and, 93, 94, 97
  spirituality and, 82
  withdrawing into, 99
dreams
  as analogies, 24, 25
  interdependence in, 97
dualism, 68, 85–86, 96, 97, 99,
    102
Dzigar Kongtrul Rinpoche, 44
  on analytical meditation, 42
  on appearance, 29
  on human potential, 105
  on pratityasamutpada, 63
  on spiritual path, 113
  See also *It's Up to You*
Dzogchen Ponlop Rinpoche, 64

earth seen from space, 10–11, 20,
    22
ease, desire for, 1, 2, 19, 76, 97
Einstein, Albert, 13, 61
emotions, 19, 101
  beliefs and, 66–67, 81, 91
  contraction of, 26–27
  deep-rooted clinging from, 98
  disturbing, 41, 102
  doubt and, 85
  expression of, 106
  grace and, 63

investigating, 33–34, 35, 47
rightness and, 8, 84
See also feelings
empathy, accurate, 103, 108
emptiness (*shunyata*), 65–66, 69–
    70, 90–91, 95, 96, 123n2
End of Faith, The (Harris), 3
enlightenment, 3–4, 85
equilibrium, 107, 111, 120
eternalism, 88–89, 92–93, 121. See
    also extremes, two
ethics, 66–67, 93, 94
everyday life
  awe in, 102–3
  sense of connection in, 105–6
  spirituality in, 67–68, 108,
    119–20
evolution, human, 20, 108–9
existence, 17, 22, 25, 86
  absence of true, 70
  belief in, 81
  clinging to, 98, 99
  eternalism and, 93–94, 96
  faith and, 2
  true mode of, 52
experience, 35–36, 54, 56–57,
    104, 119. See also direct
    experience
expression, interdependent, 37,
    95, 105–6, 109–12, 121,
    122. See also creative ex-
    pression
extremes, two, 92–94, 96, 97, 98,
    121

faith/faithing, 86
  and belief, distinctions be-
    tween, 78
  challenge of, 3
  cultural disillusionment in,
    75–76, 95
  in customizing spirituality, 116

investigating, 5–6, 84, 88–89, 121
Middle Way and, 99
need to examine, 2–3
nihilism as impediment to, 96
term, usages of, 1–2
unconditional, 82–83
as unconditional protection, 85
working definition of, 73–75, 119
fear
contraction and, 26, 27
emancipation from, 63
of extinction and death, 81, 91, 92, 95–96
living without, 12
fearlessness, 57, 98
feedback, 18, 20, 26, 112
feelings, 22, 24, 44. *See also* emotions
freedom, 19, 68, 85, 98, 107, 117
From Certainty to Uncertainty (Peat), 8
fullness, 78–79, 80, 81, 89, 103, 120
fundamentalism, 3, 75–76, 89–91, 102, 121, 122
Fuzzy Thinking (Kosko), 13, 14

global challenges, 19–20
grace, 5, 19, 97–99, 102, 112
basis for creating, 106
discernment and, 42
experiencing, 13
faith and, 74
as inspiration, 43, 117
interdependent expression and, 61
living in, 121
open-dimensionality and, 63
reification and, 104–5
relationship and, 95

as sanity, 20, 66
searching for, 111
source of, 13
in spirituality, 89
through language and communication, 114
through ritual and form, 115
gratitude, 61, 117
Gross, Terry, 9
Guenther, Herbert, 31

habit/habitual tendency, 4, 19, 33–34, 36, 47. *See also under* mind
happiness, 19, 41, 85, 120
Harris, Sam, 3
Harvard Divinity School, 13
Heart Sutra, 70, 98, 114
here, notion of, 38–39
hopelessness, 95, 101, 103
hopes and fears, 97, 103
human potential, 5, 105
humility, 9
in analytical meditation, 42–43, 49
faith and, 73, 74
grace and, 117
in investigation, 34–35
letting go into, 76
of Middle Way, 98–99
nihilism and, 95
sacredness of, 13
in understanding pratityasamutpada, 64

ignorance, 64, 97
illusion/illusory nature, 25, 32, 39, 57, 63, 66, 91
imagination, 61
impermanence, 54, 56, 57. *See also* change
India, 4, 78, 79, 114

73–74, 88, 94
loosening practice, 39–43, 95. *See also* analytical meditation
Lorenz, Edward, 61
love, 77, 105, 107, 111

Macy, Joanna, 16, 18, 119
Madhyamaka. *See* Middle Way (Madhyamaka)
magic, 24, 38, 57, 62–63, 64, 68, 95, 99
Mahayana, 66, 68, 106–9
Markel, Peggy, 59, 60
meditation, 11, 34, 67, 114, 120. *See also* analytical meditation
Melville, Herman, 44
memory, 50, 61, 106
Middle Way (Madhyamaka), 116
    autonomy, view of in, 62
    insight of, 57
    investigative path of, 34
    Nagarjuna's role in, 68
    as open inquiry, 118
    peace and, 120
    permanent self, view of in, 50–51
    purpose of, 36, 70
    as way of being, 98–99
mind
    activity of, 41
    agility of, 9, 10, 32
    assumptions about, 28
    belief and, 77
    habitual, 12–13, 57
    and heart, connection between, 107
    nature of, 39, 118
    poised for insight, 5, 84
    subjective, self as, 53, 57
Mipham Rinpoche, Je, 67–68
Mitchell, Edgar, 11

Monet, Claude, 14
Monet-Palaci, Cristina, 94
monks, story of two upon hearing of emptiness, 90–91, 94
Mother Teresa, 82–83, 85
mutual causality, 39, 88, 102, 111, 119
mutual dependency, 16, 111

Nagarjuna, 4–5, 42, 68–71, 86, 96
nature of things, 71, 73, 95
    and appearance, distinguishing, 25, 67, 69
    as dynamic, 5, 77
    as fathomless and unfixable, 96, 104, 107–9
    as illusory, 57, 63
    as interdependent, 49
    karma and, 110
    living in accord with, 117–18, 120
    misunderstanding, 75
    open-dimensionality of, 66, 110
    as unfindable, 64–65
New Testament, 78
nihilism, 91–96, 94–96, 121. *See also* extremes, two
nikayas, five, 123n2
nothingness, 91–92

O'Brian, Tom, 54
ontology, 86–88
open inquiry, 90, 118
open-dimensionality, 31–32, 34, 74
    absolute truth and, 69
    as emptiness, 66
    enjoying, 63
    in everyday life, 67–68
    karma and, 110
    perceiving, 41
open-mindedness, 9, 84, 104

openness, 9, 34
  confidence founded on, 75
  deprivation of, 102
  discernment and, 119
  grace and, 117
  of Middle Way, 98–99
  mind of complete, 5
  qualities of, 32

Padmasambhava, 79–80
pain, 17–18, 25, 31–32, 38, 47,
  97, 120
Pali Tipitaka, 123n2
peace, 89, 98, 107, 111, 120
Peat, F. David, 8, 109, 115
perceptions, 14, 112, 119
  accurate, 32
  collective, 23–24
  in distinguishing reality, 21,
    22–23
  doubting, 31
  interdependence and, 16–17
  objects of, 53
  trauma and, 27–28
perfect, nondual experience of,
    102, 103–5, 112
perfection, notion of absolute, 101
permanence, 41–42, 43, 50, 61,
    65, 75, 81
playful experimentation, 111–12
political correctness, 102
prajna, 41–42, 46–47, 71. See also
    discernment
prajna aparadha, 18
pratityasamutpada, 3–4, 89, 97
  awe in experiencing, 63–64
  benefits of understanding, 64
  choice and, 109–12
  contraction as opposite of, 26
  direct relationship with, 38–39
  eternalism and, 89
  evolution in context of, 109

faith and, 74–75
investigating, 4–6, 18
misunderstandings about,
    90–91
Nagarjuna's view of, 68–71
natural relationship with, 18
path of, 28, 120–21
respecting, 34
three analytical methods for
    understanding, 42–43
translations of term, 15–16
two scriptural uses of term,
    123n2
See also interdependence
present moment, locating, 55, 56
pride, 84, 104

reactivity, 25, 27, 33–34, 63, 69,
    83, 102–3
realization, 113–14
reasoning, 93
reification, 75, 102–3, 104
reincarnation, 77, 81
relationship
  contraction in, 26
  emptiness and, 65–66
  harmony in, 111
  nature of, 15–17
  power of, 91
  purpose of, 95
  ultimate truth and, 89
  to world, 19, 20, 23, 42
relaxation, 12–13, 36, 62
religion
  belief, understanding of in, 78
  disillusionment with, 95
  meanings of, 3
  organized, 115–18
  origins of, 99
  See also wisdom traditions
respect, 34, 36, 78, 105
responsiveness, 103, 105–6, 107–8

rightness, 8–9, 103, 104
    Buddhist path and, 88–89
    clinging/holding on to, 75–76,
        115
    freedom from, 75
    momentum of, 25
    not clinging to, 66
    protection from, 102
    questioning, 28, 30–31
    securing, 80–81
    withdrawing into, 99
    ritual and form, 113–15

sacredness, 13, 83, 91, 114
Sagan, Carl, 58, 59, 60, 62, 88
samsara, 109
sanity, 20, 66
science, 7–8, 23–24, 34–35, 43, 87,
        91, 116
scientific materialism, 93, 95
scientific rationality, 78–79
scripture, 108–9, 113, 114
security, 2, 3, 75, 86, 89, 97
self, 50–54, 61, 81, 120
self-absorption, 19, 20
self-awareness, 11
self-deception, 83
sensual world, 114–15
service, 108–9
Shantarakshita, 42
Shantideva, 39, 42, 98, 106
Shariputra, 70
singularity, 41–42, 43, 44–46,
        48–49, 61, 65, 75, 81
skepticism, 84
skillful means, 108
spiritual path, 74, 90
    Buddha's discovery of, 112
    connection to, 85
    humanness as purpose of, 86
    Middle Way as, 99
    scripture and realization as-

pects of, 113–15
spiritual teachers, 117, 118
spirituality
    and analysis, connection be-
        tween, 39–41
    customizing, danger of, 116–18
    in everyday life, 67–68, 108,
        119–20
    faith and, 3
    stagnation of, 115–16
    and temporality, separating,
        67–68
    stress, 26–27, 46, 75, 81
suffering, 19, 39, 64, 85, 107, 120,
        123n2

tender heart, 57, 103
tenderness, 12, 19, 38, 103, 105,
        107, 113
Teresa of Calcutta, Saint. *See*
        Mother Teresa
terrorism, 3
Theravada Buddhism, 123n2
Thich Nhat Hanh, 116
thingness, 49
    analyzing, 45–46
    clinging to, freedom from, 57
    distinct aspects of, 70–71
    identifying with, 47
    nominal designation and, 44
    purpose of investigating, 46,
        73–74
    See also nature of things
Thinley Norbu Rinpoche, 2
thoughts, 30
    expression of, 37, 106
    as imaginary, 61
    in investigation, 46–47
    limitations of, 44–45
    nature of, 34
    power of, 76
Tibetan Buddhism, 11, 79–80

ABOUT THE AUTHOR

Elizabeth Mattis Namgyel has studied and practiced the ancient wisdom of Mahayana Buddhism as well as the Vajrayana tradition of the Longchen Nyingthik for more than thirty years under the guidance of her teacher and husband, Dzigar Kongtrul Rinpoche. After meeting Rinpoche in Nepal in 1985, she became his first Western student and has been intimately involved with his work in bringing Buddhist wisdom to the West, particularly in the development of Mangala Shri Bhuti, an organization dedicated to the study and practice of the Longchen Nyingthik lineage. She is also a founding member and teacher of Wilderness Dharma Movement, and she is on the advisory boards of the Prison Mindfulness Network and the Buddhist Arts and Film Festival. Elizabeth has an academic background in both anthropology and Buddhist studies, but her learning is grounded above all in practice. After her many years of solitary retreat, Dzigar Kongtrul Rinpoche appointed Elizabeth retreat master at Longchen Jigme Samten Ling, Mangala Shri Bhuti's retreat center in southern Colorado. Elizabeth has edited Kongtrul Rinpoche's two books, *It's Up to You* and *Light Comes Through*, and she is the author of *The Power of an Open Question: The Buddha's Path to Freedom*. She teaches the Buddhadharma throughout the United States and Europe. More information about Elizabeth, including a schedule of her upcoming teachings and retreats, can be found at her website: www.ElizabethMattisNamgyel.com.